GOD USES *the* UNUSABLE

CARRI OLLER

ISBN: 1548029483
ISBN-13: 978-1548029487

Dedicated to
my loving Savior, first and foremost;
the love of my life and sweet husband, Matt;
my son, Abram, and daughter, Hallie;
my mom, Judy, and dad, Irmon;
my brother, Robert, and sister-in-love, Vanessa;
my nephew, Tanner;
my nieces, Tiffani, Courtney, Morgan, Kaylee, and Brylee; and
all of my family and friends.

Thank you for loving me in spite of my shortcomings
and believing in me.
Thank you for the many talks we've had, helping me decide
what I want to do with my life.
Thank you for being there for me.
Thank you for simply being you.
I love you all so much.

CONTENTS

1   God Uses Me   1

2   God Uses the Abused: Joseph   11

3   God Uses the Doubter: Gideon   31

4   God Uses the Broken: Naomi   46

5   God Uses the Sinner: David   61

6   God Uses the Unwilling: Jonah   74

7   God Uses the Fearful: Peter   86

8   God Uses the Worrier: Martha   98

9   God Uses the Hypocrite: Paul   110

10 God Can Use You, Too!   124

CHAPTER 1

Hi, I'm Carri. I'm an imperfect person who messes up on a daily basis. I doubt more often than I trust. I gripe more often than I praise. I turn to other people and things to bring me comfort and peace instead of Jesus. I sin even when I know I shouldn't. I'm simply unusable in my own eyes, and sometimes, by the world's standards, I'm unusable. I have always wondered why God uses certain people. For myself, I have always asked, "God, why are you using ME?" Maybe you can relate. Here is a piece of my story.

THE UGLY DUCKLING

In middle school, I went through that ugly duckling stage that many people go through—you know, where your body is disproportional because you are still developing and everything is just awkward. I was chubbier and more developed than most of my friends and taller than all of my friends and most of the boys in my grade. My friends were cute and dainty, and I was just, well, me. I was insecure and unsure of myself, and I definitely wasn't comfortable in my own skin.

I remember sitting in the bleachers with my friends during an assembly. We made it a point to sit close to the cutest boys in our grade because we were totally boy crazy. You know what I'm talking about? If you even catch a whiff of their mismatched cologne and aftershave—which they don't really need because they only have peach fuzz on their face—you can barely breathe because of the insane amount, but you start to melt anyway.

I spent my time during the assembly admiring God's handiwork on one of the most popular boys in our grade. I was trying to give him that "how YOU doin'" look. I even tried winking at Mr. Popular, which I'm sure just looked like I had something in my eye.

As we were slowly being dismissed, one of my best friends was flirting with these boys. Instead of being myself, I chimed in and tried to copy my friend by talking in a high-pitched, flirtatious voice.

Mr. Popular looked me over and said in front of everyone, "You are too ugly to look at and too fat to live." He then followed that hurtful and embarrassing remark by telling me, "You should go and kill yourself."

I just sat there. I felt as though I was under a magnifying glass and everyone was staring at me. His words devastated me beyond belief. I thought that my world was completely over, all because of one person's opinion about who I was. I wrote a letter to one of my best friends telling her my plans.

I was not going to be at school the next day. I was going to kill myself.

SOMETHING MISSING

I had planned to slit my wrists or take several different medications to do the job. Thankfully, my friend took the note to the school counselor, and the school counselor told my parents. They were also devastated beyond belief. They had no idea that their baby girl had so much turmoil going on inside of her.

I guess you could say that I hid my feelings well; after all, I am an actress. I was always smiling or laughing, but secretly I felt so unworthy of anyone's love and so insignificant. Even though I had a family who loved and adored me, I still felt something missing—I didn't realize at the time that I was hungry and longing for my Savior's love and affirmation.

My parents called my youth pastor and mentor after getting the news, and he counseled me. You gotta love how everything goes full circle because as I am writing this book, he and his wife are some of my dearest friends and I'm the youth pastor at his church. After much counsel and many prayers, God freed me from the false thinking that I needed to end my life because I felt that I wasn't good enough.

THE TROUBLE WITH FEELINGS

By my senior year of high school, I was known as the "Jesus Freak," which I totally took as a compliment. My passion for God kept growing and growing. By the end of my senior year, I was already on staff at my home church as the preschool pastor's assistant. I was so excited to be in ministry, but at the same time I felt as though I wasn't usable.

Ever since that time in middle school, Satan has tried to whisper lies and defeat over my life. Anytime I would take a leap forward in my faith, he would attempt with all his might to shake and break me and make me want to take a few steps backward by placing doubt and fear on my mind and my heart. I'm definitely a "feeler." Even now as an adult, I continually have to pray over my thinking (my mind) and my feelings (my heart) and align them with God's truth. I can get myself into trouble if I base my decisions on my feelings.

A VISION AND A CALLING

Fast forward to when I was twenty-one, almost twenty-two years old. My husband, son, in-loves (a.k.a. in-laws), and I were on a road trip to Florida, and I was pregnant with my daughter, Hallie. I remember my sweet and precious mommy-in-love telling me, "Just lay down in the back of the van and take a nap!" She said she would entertain my one-year-old son so that I could rest. She absolutely loved to spoil and love on her grandbabies. (She's in heaven now, and we miss her so much every day.)

As I was laying in the back seat, I was closing my eyes and trying to block out the *Dora the Explorer* and *Go, Diego, Go* episodes my son was watching for the one millionth, billionth time. I didn't realize that this moment of solitude in the backseat would be the first time I truly felt God speak to me.

It's interesting that God would impregnate me with a vision when I was actually physically pregnant with my sweet baby girl. This vision would forever fuel, shake, and change me.

I saw myself with a hands-free microphone and Bible in hand, on a large platform with other like-minded men and women Christian leaders. We were preaching to a crowd of thousands and thousands of people. Everyone there knew my name and ministry.

God revealed to me in this vision that the calling on my life was to encourage, inspire, and love people from all walks of life through the gifts and ministry He was going to give me. God was going to use me!

I started snickering in the backseat. I was thinking, "Wait a minute, God . . . Are you sure you have the right person?" Right then and there, I started making excuses for why I wasn't able. After all, I was just a sinful and broken twenty-one-year-old pregnant blonde who didn't even have a college degree! #letsjustputitalloutthere

NO EXCUSES!

I'm going to be transparent with you. Even after God gave me this vision, I have wrestled with doubt and fear every step of the way. I delayed it as long as I possibly could because I was having a hard time believing God would use a person like me. I kept making excuses. I kept speaking negativity over myself. I also allowed others who wrestled with doubts and fears speak death over the vision God gave me.

After ten years of ministry and running from the call, I felt God tugging at my heart, reminding me and shifting my focus to the vision He gave me when I was twenty-one and pregnant with my daughter. He was calling me to pursue writing, public speaking, and acting. He wanted to use me to be a different voice for Him, one that was bold, funny, and loving. Once again, I literally laughed out loud and said, "God, I really think you have the wrong person! Something must be a little off because I am not usable in any of those ways!" As if God could really mess up! I had another long list of excuses for why I was incapable of doing what He was wanting me to do.

God kept bringing me back to the vision, and no matter how much I battled and tried to run from the vision, it kept chasing after me. He didn't want me to settle. He didn't want me to believe the lies. Everywhere I would look, there would be confirmation after confirmation after confirmation pointing me back toward the vision. I couldn't outrun the call on my life; God wouldn't let me. I tried. God always wins—shocking, I know. #sarcasm

So, I finally started taking baby steps and stopped making so many excuses. God then started opening doors that I couldn't have opened myself. He started setting up divine appointments with people in the Christian entertainment industry. I definitely, absolutely, can't take any credit for those. He was chiseling away my insecurities. He was shaping me to be the woman He knew I was, the woman He wanted me to be.

Through everything, I have learned that God seeks out the ones people often overlook. He doesn't need to look for perfect because He's perfect.

ALWAYS BY YOUR SIDE

Becoming a mom has helped me truly appreciate what my parents have done for me and also, on a much bigger scale, what God has done for me. My kids are my heart. I love and adore them; I would do anything for them. I want to provide the best for them. I want to watch them flourish in this world.

My son, Abram, has high-functioning autism and sensory processing disorder, making social interaction as well as some large and small motor skills a little more difficult for him than they are for everyone else. I remember when Abram was playing football, he was getting discouraged because he couldn't run like everyone else. We do that, don't we? We look at other people's races, other people's lives, and compare their race with ours.

All the other parents were sitting there talking and having a leisurely time as their sons were out hustling at practice. When I saw my son struggle and get discouraged, I immediately ran out there as quickly as I could in my flip-flops and started running laps with him. I know I looked absolutely crazy! Mind you, I wasn't in the best of shape and, at one point, I wanted to throw up from running so much. But I couldn't quit on my son, so I kept going. I told him, "You can do it! I'm right here with you!" I wasn't going to leave his side. When Abram knew I was there with him, he took his eyes off of everyone else and finished strong.

As a mom, I want to try to cover all the potholes in my children's lives, but I know I can't. They will make their mistakes because they are human just like me, just like you, and just like all the people in this book. However, I will do everything I can to encourage them to believe in themselves and more importantly, believe in the One who created them in the first place. Thinking about what my heart is for my children puts in perspective what God really wants for His children.

God doesn't want to see you become discouraged or paralyzed by anxiety, thinking that He can't or won't use you. God gives you the freedom of choice. God is always there to catch you or cheer you on, and He definitely wants to use you in mighty ways to bring Him glory.

WANTED: YOU

In this book, we are going to look at people from the Bible whom you might not think God would be able to use for big purposes because they don't fit the mold. He sees them differently through His perfect view instead of the world's defective and skewed view, and He sees you differently, too.

He sees the full, big picture of your life when you only see little pieces at a time.

He sees past your flaws and mistakes.

He sees His Son Jesus in you.

And He wants to use you for His kingdom. He wants to stretch you in ways you never thought possible and challenge you in ways you've never dreamed. He wants to grow your faith as you trust in Him. He wants to bless you. He loves and cares about every single detail in your life, the big details and the small details. Just like I was there with my son, Abram, He's right there with you as you run this race we call life (except God doesn't get tired of running and He's always in shape).

The question is, are you going to allow Him to do what He wants to do in your life? Are you willing to be stretched in ways you never dreamed possible? Are you willing to have faith the size of a mustard seed and watch God show off and move mountains in your life? Are you willing to be used by God? If so, then continue reading this book and allow God to free you from what might be holding you back from reaching God's best for you. Because, believe it or not, God wants to do a good work in you and through you. YOU ARE USABLE!

CHAPTER 2

God Uses the Abused: Joseph

Genesis 37–50

Of the people I've known in my life who have experienced some form of abuse, all of them have said to me something like, "God can't use me because of my past and the ugliness of abuse in my life. Because it was so ugly, I'm now ugly, unlovable, and unusable." They see the ugliness as a label that stays on them, tainting them and causing them to be unusable. They think that they are too worn and broken to be used by God in any capacity. It breaks my heart. I want you to understand that if you are there right now, that's simply a huge, ugly lie. Unfortunately, so many people out there believe that lie. You need to hear that GOD USES THE ABUSED! If we allow Him, He will use all of our hurts and offenses, including abuse, as a microphone to elevate our voices and help those around us.

The story of Joseph is a powerful example of forgiving your abusers. Joseph encountered abuse from his family, those in higher power, and those who simply wanted to cause him strife and pain because of their own agendas and impure, selfish motives. The story starts with a coat, and it is only the beginning of a long—and I mean LONG—thirteen-year journey.

Joseph was one of the youngest sons of Jacob, and Jacob loved him more than his brothers. Jacob gave Joseph a coat of many colors, which further displayed his favoritism toward Joseph. Joseph was overconfident because of the favor he was shown and became a walking target for his brothers.

DREAMS AND DOUBTS

When he was seventeen years old, Joseph had dreams given to him by the Lord. These dreams were a small glimpse of Joseph's future, and by glimpse, I mean a small piece of the puzzle in his journey. In Genesis 37:5–7 (MSG), he describes his first dream to his brothers: "We were all out in the field gathering bundles of wheat. All of a sudden my bundle stood straight up and your bundles circled around it and bowed down to mine." Then he says, "I dreamed another dream—the sun and moon and eleven stars bowed down to me!" (Genesis 37:9, MSG). His brothers mocked him and told him that he was out of his mind if he thought that they would bow down to their little brother!

Isn't that the truth? When God gives you a dream or a vision, the doubters who seem to speak the loudest are the ones closest to you, even the ones you love the most in the world: your spouse, parents, siblings, other family members, friends, and mentors. I've had that happen several times. When God gave me a dream or a vision, I would tell someone closest to me, and this person would respond with, "Are you sure that's what God said? Are you really listening to God or to yourself?" [That's why it's important not to get validation from people, but to seek God first and foremost for His clarity.] Unfortunately, people tend to listen to people instead of listening to their Heavenly Father who gave them the dream or vision in the first place. I think many of us wouldn't be so confused on our journey if we simply turned down the static in our lives (people) and turned up the truth (God and His word). *True*

Even with the spoken doubts from his family, Joseph held on tightly to the dreams God put in his heart.

THE GREEN-EYED MONSTER

Unfortunately for Joseph, his brothers had a jealousy problem, a huge one actually. His brothers' jealousy grew into hate, so much so that they wanted to kill him. I'm not talking about that expression when someone says, "I'm going to kill you!" No, they literally plotted to kill him.

One day Joseph's brothers came up with a devious plan to kill him; they wanted him to die, but his brother Reuben wouldn't let that happen and instead convinced them to put Joseph in a dried-up cistern. However, this cruel plan meant for evil would be used as a stepping stone toward anointing and empowerment in accomplishing God's purpose for him.

I'm sure you have encountered jealous people in your life. Lord knows I have, several times! You know, those people who see your anointing and favor and hate the fact that you are walking in peace and obedience, using your talents for the Lord, so they attempt to distract and discourage you from going toward your purpose because they are too afraid to go toward their own purpose! #dropthemic

GOD'S PERFECT TIMING

Instead, Joseph's brothers sold him into slavery and told their father, Jacob, that Joseph was dead. An Egyptian man named Potiphar became his master. Joseph gained Potiphar's trust, and he eventually became Potiphar's right-hand man. But Potiphar's wife lusted after Joseph—apparently Joseph was a good-looking dude. She approached Joseph and asked him to sleep with her. Sounds like a soap opera, doesn't it? Joseph denied her advances because he didn't want to dishonor Potiphar and, more importantly, God. He ran from Potiphar's wife, and she tore a piece of his clothing. She falsely claimed that Joseph had raped her.

Joseph then gets thrown into jail for raping a woman he didn't rape. There in jail he ends up interpreting the dreams of two people who worked for Pharaoh and were also in jail: the cupbearer and the baker. Joseph interpreted the cupbearer's dream as good news that the cupbearer would get his job back; he interpreted the baker's dream as a death sentence. Both dreams came true. As the cupbearer left prison, Joseph pleaded with him: "Remember me!" The man forgot him for a while until, in God's perfect timing, Joseph was remembered.

Of course, we know that God never forgot Joseph; God knew what was going to unfold in Joseph's life. Joseph ended up interpreting dreams for the Pharaoh. These dreams prophesied a famine in Egypt, and eventually Pharaoh put Joseph second in command over all Egypt in preparation. Joseph did everything with excellence and was obedient in the little things until God fulfilled the big dream for Joseph.

I've seen it time and time again. God always exposes the darkness and impure motives of those doing wrong, myself included. There are consequences for those who do wrong; He uplifts the ones doing right in His perfect timing.

TRUE COLORS

As with the other dreams, Pharaoh's dream about the famine came true. During the famine, Joseph's brothers traveled to Egypt, but they didn't recognize Joseph because he was decked out in Egyptian gear and even spoke a different language. But Joseph definitely recognized them. Joseph then understood the dream that

God gave him when he was seventeen years old. The pieces were falling into place. The dream about his brothers bowing down to him came true.

When Joseph's brothers realized who Joseph was, they wept and wept. They were so broken, and they had carried this burden of their own actions for so long. It robbed them of thirteen years of complete happiness, peace, and joy. It also caused them to miss out on having a relationship with Joseph. I'm sure they were embarrassed because of their choices.

Joseph could have had his brothers thrown into jail or even killed—he had the power and authority to do so. He could have had them experience the thirteen-year hell that he went through. However, his response to them is mind-blowing because he said to his brothers: "'Don't be afraid. Am I in the place of God? You intended to harm me, but God intended it for good to accomplish what is now being done, the saving of many lives. So then, don't be afraid. I will provide for you and your children.' And he reassured them and spoke kindly to them" (Genesis 50:19–21, NIV).

Wow. Wow. Wow. That's all I can say when reading that scripture. How many of us would respond that way to our offenders? How many of us would reassure and talk kindly to the ones who did the exact opposite to us? How many of us would offer blessings to those who have greatly hurt us and even cursed us? I'll take a bet and say most of us would probably come up with plans to get even with our brothers for the hardships and brokenness they put us through.

Forgiveness goes against our sinful flesh. It definitely goes against what the world teaches. We have that cye-for-an-eye mentality; we feel entitled because they hurt us, so we think that we should hurt them back. Jesus tells us to do the opposite and turn the other cheek.

What Joseph does when he sees his brothers is truly remarkable. He displayed the love of Christ by forgiving his brothers. It is a picture of forgiveness with no strings attached. He showed what it means to have your faith life forced into the open to show its true colors.

JOURNEY TO THE DESTINATION

I admire how Joseph knew the dream God placed in his heart, and even when he was abused and all hell broke loose and his journey to the destination took thirteen years, he saw God in the details, stoplights, and detours. He didn't turn against God; he ran toward Him. He didn't allow the hurt and anguish of abuse to trap him in a place of resentment and bitterness. With all of these twists and turns and round-bouts in Joseph's story, his faith in God's goodness never wavered. He held onto the truth. He knew that this wasn't the end of his story.

You may be going through something right now. You might even think the end of your story is here and there's simply no hope left. But can I encourage you with this truth? God has the final say. It's not over until He says it's over.

You see, God gave Joseph a glimpse into the future so that Joseph would have hope. I think God gives us dreams and visions to hold onto so when we are in the desert, the barren lands, and the wilderness, so when we feel tired, weak, and want to give up, we can continue taking strides toward our purpose. Hold onto hope!

There have been a few times in my life where instead of running toward God when things weren't working out, I actually ran towards myself. I had myself on my mind all the time. In my selfishness and ambition, I thought that I could do a better job than God because God wasn't getting me to the destination fast enough. But when I finally submitted to God's will and relied on His strength and not my own, there would be breakthrough, peace, and joy that could only be from God.

God would be an unjust God if He gave us something we weren't ready for. He would also be unjust if He didn't give us something we WERE ready for. Many of us hate the process, but we have to go through the process to appreciate the destination. For Joseph, going through this painful process of abuse made him the leader he needed to be when he reached the destination. God loves us too much to not grow us in character first. What the devil intends for bad, God always uses for good.

FORGIVENESS AS A CHOICE

My dad is my hero and another amazing example of forgiveness. He has a quiet and gentle spirit but is also a goofy, fun-loving, witty comedian with the absolute best dry sense of humor. He makes me laugh so hard that my stomach hurts, I have tears rolling down my cheeks (and sometimes pee down my legs—yes, I've peed my pants on a few occasions), and I start snorting uncontrollably (yes, it's true, I snort when I laugh). He reads his Bible every morning. He literally gets on his knees and lifts his Bible up in the air and fervently prays for everything from his wife, children, and grandchildren to his job, health, finances, and more.

In my dad's case, the offenders were his parents. You see, my dad was adopted. He didn't get to meet his biological parents until he was a grown man with a wife and family of his own. I can only imagine all the questions my dad had for them: Why would you give me away? Didn't you want me? Didn't you love me? What was wrong with me?

My mom was a go-getter and did some investigations that led my parents to my grandpa. One day both my parents went to my grandpa's house without permission and knocked on his front door. My dad didn't reveal who he was, but he did ask if my grandpa knew my grandmother. My grandpa acted like he didn't know her at first. But my mom, being the bold, superstar detective that she is, said, "You know you were married to her. This is your marriage certificate right here!" With wide eyes, he admitted that he knew my grandma and told them he believed she lived in Texas. My parents tracked my grandma down, and my grandpa played a key role in making it happen.

The first time my dad met his biological mother, she was afraid that he was going to hit her or belittle her because that was her life experience thus far. However, my dad did the unexpected to my grandma: he took a deep breath, straightened his tie, and then opened his strong arms and walked toward his mom to embrace her with kindness, gentleness, and love. It's one of those moments where you hope and pray you would display the same Christ-like character given the opportunity.

My grandma confirmed who my dad's biological father was. After that, my parents went to see him again and let him know he had a son. My grandpa was shocked! He asked my dad, "Why didn't you tell me this the last time I saw you?" They explained that they wanted to talk with my grandma first to be sure he was indeed the father. With love in his eyes, he looked my dad over, examining their similarities like parents do when they see their child for the first time. It was such a sweet moment.

As they developed a relationship, my dad had a chance to talk with my grandpa about the Lord. For my dad, it was more important to make sure he knew where my grandpa would spend eternity than it was to yell at him or act resentful of his choices. My dad also got to lead his mom to Jesus, and he even officiated her funeral. Although they didn't get a lot of time together here on earth, my sweet daddy and his biological parents will get to spend eternity together in heaven.

Wow. Wow. Wow. Yes, I said it again. You see, my dad chose not only to forgive his parents, but also he chose to free future generations by breaking the curse and cycle of rejection and abandonment. He made an intentional choice about what kind of man, what kind of husband, and what kind of father he was going to be. He decided that he wanted to be a man who pursued God in every detail of his life, and for that, I am forever grateful. He didn't want to abandon his children. He wanted to make sure we had what we needed and, many times, what we wanted. He wanted to be a good example of what a gentleman looked like toward my sweet momma, my brother, and me. He did not allow unforgiveness to have power over his life.

Through the years of being in ministry, I've seen many people go through horrible and traumatic situations caused by family members, trusted friends, or sometimes even perfect strangers. I have witnessed people choose to stay a victim and run from the problem. They choose to live in the wilderness of unforgiveness. They allow themselves to stay and be consumed in such a deep, dark place of despair, making everything and everyone around them feel the heaviness and darkness that surrounds, shackles, and enslaves them. They become an island from everyone, which isn't healthy or good for anyone. But I have also witnessed some of those people choose to be better, not bitter. They rise above the ashes and choose to forgive.

BREAKING NEWS!

You see, people are people. They aren't perfect. We put so much trust, faith, and hope in people and get mad and discouraged when these people turn out to be imperfect. We give people too much credit. No matter if you are part of a family, school, business, church, or ministry, you will eventually run into someone who will let you down and even hurt you, unintentionally and sometimes intentionally. Why? Because people aren't God. God won't let you down. God is the only constant one who keeps His promises and works for your good.

I've seen people jump from church family to church family because they got hurt by other people. I've also seen people stop going to church altogether because they allowed other people's shortcomings to dictate their feelings regarding church. They couldn't stand how people at churches were hypocrites, but AREN'T WE ALL HYPOCRITES? Church isn't a place for the healthy; it's for the sick, the lost, and the broken. Because, truth be told, we are all in desperate need of healing and restoration in some area of our lives. "We" includes pastors, ministry leaders, and volunteers. Don't believe the lies of the evil one that you can't attend church because church is a place where you got hurt.

As Christians, we preach a message of love and forgiveness, yet we can't practice what we preach. We need to forgive. If we don't, we are allowing the body of Christ to be ripped and torn apart, which makes us easier targets for the evil one to wipe out.

We are stronger together than we are apart. We need to be united, not divided. Just something to think about . . . .

TAKING POISON, DRIVING OFF CLIFFS, AND CARRYING AROUND DEAD CORPSES

I guarantee that you have at least one person in your life right now you need to forgive. In fact, I bet that as you are reading this you can think of at least five people in your life right now you need to forgive. God wants you to be freed from the burden of unforgiveness. One of my dear friends, Christian author and speaker Christy Johnson (a.k.a. my "Big Sister") showed me that when you type the word unforgiveness it will keep highlighting in red because the dictionary doesn't even have the word unforgiveness in it. Unforgiveness is a man-made word, a man-made action.

Even when we choose not to forgive, God is a God of forgiveness. Not only does He want us to know we are forgiven, but He wants us to forgive others who have done us wrong. He wants us to forgive our abusers.

When you don't forgive, all you are doing is hurting yourself. It would be like drinking poison and expecting it to hurt someone else when all it would really do is hurt and destroy you. Or it would be like driving a car off of the cliff and expecting it to hurt another person when you're the only one in the car. Unforgiveness is like carrying a dead corpse around with you everywhere you go.

It stinks, it's gross, it's heavy, and it slows you down. God wants you to experience life in abundance, but how can you do that if you insist on carrying that heavy burden everywhere you go? It truly doesn't even make sense to not forgive.

I know someone who turned into salt and didn't get to see everything God had for her because she wasn't willing to let go of what was behind her (her past) to see the blessings in front of her (her future.) If you think I'm crazy for saying that, look it up in Genesis 19. Lot's wife literally turns into salt.

Don't allow yourself to be trapped in a prison when you should be running free. It is crazy that even though most of us know we can be and are free in Jesus, we choose to get in the jail cell of anger and bitterness, shut the door, and lock and throw away the key. So many of us waste so much of our time hating and trying to get even with our abusers and offenders instead of praying for them, forgiving them, and allowing God to heal us and fight our battles for us.

If only more people would understand the freedom in forgiveness, our world would look dramatically different. Yet, unfortunately, this broken world craves brokenness. God wants us to be free; that is why He sent His one and only precious Son, Jesus.

THE SUPERSTAR OF FORGIVENESS

The forgiveness story of Joseph and the forgiveness story of my dad remind me so much of Jesus. When He was hanging on the cross, He could have totally wiped out all of His abusers, but He didn't. Instead, Jesus pleaded to His Heavenly Father for His abusers, the ones who kicked Him, spit on Him, whipped Him, cursed Him, mocked Him, belittled Him, and nailed Him to the cross. He said, "Father forgive them, for they know not what they do" (Luke 23:34, ESV).

Blows. My. Mind.

Jesus is the ultimate example of forgiving the abuser. He's the superstar of forgiveness, and "in Him we have redemption through His blood, the forgiveness of sins, in accordance with the riches of God's grace" (Ephesians 1:7, NIV). He carried the sin and abuse of mankind, yet He showed amazing grace hanging on that cross. That grace was freely given, not earned.

THE REST OF MY STORY

There are many situations where it would seem impossible to forgive, but with God's strength we can. I've told you how in middle school I was bullied by one of the most popular boys in school and almost took my life because of the abuse. With lots of help and prayer, I was freed from that way of thinking. I could have stayed angry at this boy, but instead of allowing the hurt to take over, I chose to forgive him.

I can tell you that when I forgave my abuser, I was free. I mean FREE! It was as if I was in chains that shackled me into believing lies about who I was. And when I forgave—truly forgave—those chains were completely broken.

My abuser didn't have any more power over me.

In my senior year of high school, that same boy who bullied me and told me that I should go kill myself actually asked me for forgiveness and even asked me to pray for him. Because of God's grace, I was able to pray for and with my abuser. Because of God's grace, I was able to forgive the inexcusable. God has forgiven me for my offenses. So I couldn't help but want to forgive because God has graciously forgiven the inexcusable in me. God gives us the strength to give grace to the undeserving and love to the unlovable.

THE FORGIVEN MUST FORGIVE

In Matthew 6:14 (NIV), Jesus said, "For if you forgive other people when they sin against you, your heavenly Father will also forgive you." Everyone wants to be forgiven and loved. We all want God's forgiveness or forgiveness from others when we mess up or fall short. We all want grace given to us when we screw up.

But the moment someone else screws up we are so quick to point fingers, pick up rocks, and draw lines of no hope in the sand. We feel like we need to punish the other person by not forgiving. It makes us feel in control over the situation to keep score of someone else's wrongs. [Unforgiveness is pride in disguise.] Thank goodness none of us are God because we would all be in trouble.

God is an amazing Heavenly Father. He is a good judge. He is just to the just and unjust alike. He doesn't play favorites. Romans 2:1-3 (NIV) tells us,

> You therefore, have no excuse, you who pass judgment on someone else, for at whatever point you judge another, you are condemning yourself, because you who pass judgment do the same things. Now we know that God's judgment against those who do such things is based on truth. So when you, a mere human being, pass judgment on them and yet do the same things, do you think you will escape God's judgment?

How do you want to be judged? None of us are without sin. We can't throw a stone at other people because they sin differently than us. The goal of faith isn't perfection; it is simply the pursuit of Christ. How you judge is how God will judge you. Think about that the next time you are quick to judge!

WHAT WILL YOU CHOOSE?

Now, please hear me, I'm not saying that forgiving someone is easy, especially when someone did the unthinkable. It's not. Depending on the severity of the situation, it can be a long and strenuous process that requires counseling. But even still, it's not an impossibility to forgive.

Joseph had the opportunity to get even, yet he chose to be free. God used Joseph and Joseph's hard journey to save many lives, including the lives of his abusers. My dad had the opportunity to be angry and repeat the curse and cycle of rejection and abandonment, but he chose to be free. God has used my dad to lead his mom and many others to Christ and to break the generational curse of sin in his family. Jesus had the choice to free Himself or make us free through Him, and because of Jesus, we are forever FREE. I had the choice to be the victim, but I chose to be free. God has used my testimony of low self-worth and self-esteem to help free others from the same mindset.

You also have the freedom to choose to be free or a slave. What will you choose? I pray that you choose freedom. I promise you that if you choose freedom, you won't be disappointed. Who knows what beauty will come from the ashes? Think of the people you'll be able to help because you allowed yourself to be healed, to be vulnerable, to be forever free.

FOCUS VERSES

"In prayer there is a connection between what God does and what you do. You can't get forgiveness from God, for instance, without also forgiving others. If you refuse to do your part, you cut yourself off from God's part." Matthew 6:14, MSG

Live creatively friends. If someone falls into sin, forgivingly restore him, saving your critical comments for yourself. You might be needing forgiveness before the day's out. Stoop down and reach to those who are oppressed. Share their burdens and so complete Christ's law. If you think you are too good for that, you are badly deceived. Galatians 6:1, MSG

You know that under pressure your faith life is forced into the open and shows its true colors. James 1:3, MSG

QUESTIONS FOR REFLECTION

1. How do I relate to Joseph's story?

_____

_____

_____

2. Is there someone I need to forgive?

_____

3. Is there someone I need to ask forgiveness from?

_____

_____

_____

4. How can I use the obstacles and circumstances in my life for
   God's glory?

_____

_____

_____

PRAYER

After you ask yourself these questions, pray and ask God to deliver
you from unforgiveness against any abusers or offenders:

"Dear God, please help me forgive the unforgiveable. Please help
me love the unloveable. Help me see them through your eyes. Help
me love with your heart. Align my thoughts with yours. Thank
you, God, for forgiving me and loving me right where I am. I love
you, Lord. Amen."

CHAPTER 3

God Uses the Doubter: Gideon

Judges 6–8

Gideon was a military leader, judge, and prophet who had a calling to go into battle and free the people of Israel from the domination of the fake gods and idols of Midan. Now just reading that sentence, you might think to yourself, "Wow! It seems like he would be the Dwayne Johnson, Arnold Schwarzenegger, or Sylvester Stallone of the Bible." But NO. He actually wasn't like that at first. He was a doubter who made excuses for himself, questioned God constantly, and asked God to prove Himself multiple times.

A VIEW TO THE END

When God first approached Gideon through one of His angels, Gideon was just an ordinary guy, threshing and hiding wheat in a winepress to keep it from the Midianites in a nearby battle. Some bible scholars say that Gideon was scared of the fight because he wasn't out there with guns blazing, kicking butt, and taking names. Other scholars say that when the Israelites were hiding and starving themselves out of fear for their lives and the lives of their family, Gideon was the one who was out there getting food for everyone and hiding it from the enemy. He had a bold spirit and a heart of action, kind of like Robin Hood. My favorite version is the Disney one where Robin Hood is a cartoon fox. Oh, sorry about that "Carri moment"! Back to Gideon! #squirrel

Although Gideon may have been hiding from the fight, an angel of God came to him and called him a MIGHTY WARRIOR and said that God was with him. Gideon replied:

> "With *me*, my master? If God is with us, why has all this happened to us? Where are all the miracle-wonders our parents and grandparents told us about, telling us, 'Didn't God deliver us from Egypt?' The fact is, God has nothing to do with us—he has turned us over to Midian."
>
> God faced him directly: "Go in this strength that is yours. Save Israel from Midian. Haven't I just sent you?"
>
> Gideon said to him, "*Me*, my master? How and with what could I ever save Israel? Look at me. My clan's the weakest in Manasseh and I'm the runt of the liter."
>
> God said to him, "I'll be with you. Believe me, you'll defeat Midian as one man." (Judges 6:13–16, MSG)

All I can say is yowzers! That's some powerful stuff right there! God was telling Gideon that these people who have been a thorn in his side and a pain in the rear for his people are going down, and God is going to use Gideon to do it! It kind of reminds me of any movie with a spy. They receive a mission from their "boss," they are told what their mission is, and they go and execute it.

Gideon did execute his mission but with doubt and hesitation along the way. He expressed doubt on the calling of his life and doubt in his creator. He challenged God for his lack of "showing up" for His people. Gideon also complained about their circumstances and hardships. I'm sure you have never done that before. #hahayeahright

It can be hard for people to see themselves the way God sees them. But this is what I love about God: He sees the finished product in us when we are still in the testing and dreaming stage. He sees the big picture; we can only see a little bit of the picture at a time. I think God limits our view to protect us from getting overwhelmed because if we knew every single thing that would happen, good or bad, we might throw up our white flags and quit before reaching the finish line.

You have probably looked in the mirror and thought horrible lies about yourself. I bet if someone would talk to you the way that you talk to yourself, you would probably karate chop them in the jugular. (I don't know why, but that's my favorite saying!) I know that I have spoken horrible lies about myself. We are all human and allow the enemy to creep into our lives and whisper doubt.

Gideon was called a mighty warrior because that was who the God of the universe designed him to be. God created each of us on purpose for a specific purpose. What a humbling and amazing thought! How can we doubt the call on our lives when it comes from the One who designed us? It takes courage to obey God in spite of our doubts. But when you begin to understand what God has designed you to do and see your God-given potential, you will become courageous.

ENOUGH IS ENOUGH!

Not only did Gideon make up excuses and question God, but he also kept asking God to give him signs to show that He would be there to back Gideon and to confirm what He had asked Gideon to do.

Wait. What?

Yes, immediately after God first spoke with him, "Gideon said, 'If you're serious about this, do me a favor: Give me a sign to back up what you are telling me. Don't leave until I come back and bring you my gift.' He [God] said, 'I'll wait till you get back'" (Judges 6:17–18, MSG). Okay, so not only did Gideon tell God to prove Himself, but he also told God to wait. Gideon straight up put God on hold! I don't know about you, but it drives me nuts when I call a business, and they put me on hold for what seems like an eternity. Gideon put God on hold and didn't even have strange music playing while he did it.

For his gift, Gideon then went and prepared a young goat and bread made without yeast and set it all before God on a rock, as the angel of God instructed him to do. The angel touched the meat and bread with a stick, and it instantly caught on fire. Gideon was amazed.

When I first read the story of Gideon, I thought to myself, "What an idiot!" He is face-to-face with the angel of God, and it isn't enough for him? I can imagine God clearing His throat gently, giving me a look, and saying something like, "Really, Carri? Really? How many times have you done that, my dear?" We are all a lot like Gideon. We read God's word, and even believe God's word, but when the moment comes and God tells us to do something that might be bizarre or impossible, we doubt the very words God speaks to us.

God gave Gideon confirmation after confirmation. At one point later on in the story, Gideon took a wool fleece and put it on the ground. He asked God to make it wet but keep the ground dry from any morning dew. The next morning, God did everything that Gideon requested. But Gideon still needed more proof before he would really believe in what God had promised! It is definitely a "doubting Thomas" situation. Gideon then said to God, "Do not be angry with me. Let me make just *one more request* [emphasis added]. Allow me one more test with the fleece, but this time make the fleece dry and let the ground be covered with dew" (Judges 6:39, NIV). We see Gideon have God perform this miracle, too!

God was being crystal clear. He is so very patient with us in our excuses and doubts. What a gentleman God is! He is such a good, good Father. He doesn't want us to have a half-hearted faith. He wants us to have a genuine faith.

I love how Gideon had a genuine faith in the one true God but also had to fight his fleshly doubts. I also love how God uses miracles all throughout the Bible to help his children get revelation. God still does that for us today.

THE FINAL PROOF

After these signs, Gideon finally believed God and started taking down the bricks of doubt that he had built up around himself. Then Gideon gathered an army, but guess what? God told Gideon that his army was too big. God didn't want people to take credit for the victory that He would bring. God wanted to show off, to reveal Himself to be the one true God. God wanted to break pride and replace it with humility.

Gideon followed God's instructions and cut the army from several thousands to three hundred men. Gideon and his army of only three hundred won the war, just as God had told him. At the end of it all, God got the glory that He deserved and God blessed Gideon and his family. Because of Gideon's obedience, his land had peace for forty years. I hope you read the story of Gideon in the book of Judges because it's stinking awesome!

It takes faith and trust on our part to allow God to do His part. Don't get me wrong, God could totally do whatever He wants to do without us, but because God is so faithful and good, He invites us to take part in the blessing. He's a good daddy that way. I know, personally, I want the best for my kids. When training them to do something new such as riding a bike, I know that if they give it some practice, they will be able to achieve success. I encourage them because I know they are capable even when they think they aren't. When they put in the work and trust what I'm telling them, they always achieve what they thought was simply impossible.

TRUSTING GOD IN THE BIG THINGS

When our son, Abram, was five, his pre-k teacher (a.k.a. Abram's angel) had a private conversation with me one day after class. She told me that she had some concerns about Abe. He was struggling with fine-motor and some large-motor skills as well as eye contact. She suggested that we take him in for testing to see exactly what was going on.

After that conversation, I was in complete and utter denial and angry—full of so many emotions to the point that I was losing sleep. I thought to myself, "surely not my son." But we listened to the teacher and had Abram tested. He was diagnosed with high-functioning autism and sensory processing disorder.

When I found out the diagnosis, I was frustrated with God. I remember praying and asking God to please take this away from Abram. I was doubting the diagnosis, and I was doubting my capability as a mother to support Abram in the way he needed. I was even believing lies from the enemy saying that it was my fault that Abram had autism and this disorder.

I remember sitting in the doctor's office one day, looking at other parents who were going through similar challenges. Some of their children's cases were more serious, some were similar, and some were minor. I remember this day so clearly because it was the day that I finally let go of what I thought should happen and how things should be and allowed God to give me the clarity that He was waiting on my heart to accept.

I found myself saying thank you to God for the gift of being in this doctor's office so that I could be a light to these people I normally might not have the privilege of meeting. Thank you, Lord, for the opportunity for my son to encourage these children he wouldn't normally encounter if he wasn't in this doctor's office. Thank you, Lord, for the gift of being Abram's mom because he has taught me to be an overcomer and to not be so serious about everything.

During my quiet time one day, God confirmed how autism and sensory processing disorder were a gift with these scriptures from 2 Corinthians 12:7-10 (MSG):

> Because of the extravagance of those revelations, and so I wouldn't get a big head, I was given the gift of a handicap to keep me in constant touch with my limitations. Satan's angel did his best to get me down; what he in fact did was push me to my knees. No danger then of walking around high and mighty! At first I didn't think of it as a gift, and

begged God to remove it. Three times I did that, and then he told me, "My grace is enough; it's all you need. My strength comes into its own in your weakness." Once I heard that, I was glad to let it happen. I quit focusing on the handicap and began appreciating the gift. It was a case of Christ's strength moving in on my weakness. Now I take limitations in stride, and with good cheer, these limitations that cut me down to size—abuse, accidents, opposition, bad breaks. I just let Christ take over! And so the weaker I get, the stronger I become.

What amazes me even to this day is how God gives us the exact word when we need it. We only have to be willing to listen.

Abram is almost eleven years old now, and he is doing absolutely amazing. He is super smart and very wise beyond his years. My son has never met a stranger. Every time I drop him off at school, there's always someone who says, "Hi, Abram!" He is also a little comedian. He delivers these one-liners that are so hilarious and true. He says what I sometimes wish I could say out loud. He's a hoot! I wouldn't doubt it if he has his own sitcom someday. I'm serious! Folks, be on the lookout for Abram Oller! I'm proud of the man he is becoming. I tell him all the time that God comes first, and if he keeps God first, everything else will come together. I always tell my son and my daughter to reach for the stars and follow their dreams, and don't let anyone tell them they can't because with God they CAN!

Through my son's visits to the doctor and occupational therapist, my husband has learned that he too has high-functioning autism. It has helped my husband understand himself and everything that he has experienced in his life. It has helped me understand my husband and his needs better. It has helped us both be more patient in life and honest with each other. We have all benefited from trusting God in this situation.

TRUSTING GOD IN THE SMALL THINGS

In my life, God has been faithful in the big things as well as the small things. One day I was praying and asking God to somehow provide a way for us to get hair bows for my daughter, Hallie. She liked having bows in her hair and all of her bows were worn out and falling apart. We were struggling financially and didn't have the money to go out and purchase new ones. I felt discouraged, so I prayed for hair bows.

A few days later one of our sweet neighbors sent me a text. She has a daughter a little bit older than Hallie, and she had gone through her daughter's room and cleared out a bunch of hair bows that weren't being worn anymore and were in great shape. My neighbor was texting me to ask if Hallie would want these bows! I told her: "Yes!" I started laughing, with tears running down my cheeks. Our neighbor brought a tall kitchen trash bag full of bows. I explained to her that I had literally been praying for hair bows, and God answered in a big, unexpected way.

God is detail-oriented. He is the creator of small details and cares about them just as much as we do. And God cares about us. Some might say that it would be silly to pray for something as insignificant as hair bows, but they were significant to me and God knew that! I wanted to provide my daughter with hair bows because she loved them. God definitely wants to provide for us because He loves us passionately. Never doubt that!

GROWING IN TRUST

When my husband and I are in a difficult season and trusting God seems impossible, God reminds me of these stories. Even writing this book is a faith walk. To be honest with you, right now as I'm typing this book, I don't even know how or when it will officially be published. Financially, it's not in the cards for us to self-publish. All I know is that I can't deny the call any longer. God will make a way in His perfect timing. I have gotten a taste of what God is capable of and it is much more than I could ever dream.

God has called me not only to write but also to public speaking and acting. I don't know how it all will play out, and I don't know all of the details: all I know is that I have to be obedient and let the God of the details make a way where there seems to be no way. I feel so humbled and thankful to be a note in God's song.

HOW'S YOUR FAITH?

Gideon had faith. Yes, he had his doubts, but with God he was able to overcome them. He was able to stare the enemy down and take the enemy out. He started out with excuses and ended his story knowing that God was and is faithful in all circumstances. God doesn't make excuses; He creates opportunities.

Are you one who tends to have excuses for everything? You know good and well that God told you to do something, but you're constantly in a mindset of doubt and you're too afraid to step out and do it. I can guarantee you are thinking right this moment about several times in your life where you have struggled with doubt—it could even be happening in your life right now. I have been that person more times than I would like to admit.

As God has proven Himself time and time again, I want to tell every person I come into contact with about His faithfulness and goodness. Right now He is paving the way for you to accomplish so much more than you have ever dreamed. He has designed you to be a powerful note in His song. Don't be afraid anymore. Be bold and courageous! Start doing what He's asked you to do, even if you don't have the financial backing to do so. Stop doubting. Stop making excuses. Remember, faith is knowing that something will happen without seeing it happen, before it happens.

FOCUS VERSES

Commit your way to the Lord; trust in him and he will do this. He will make your righteous reward shine like the dawn, your vindication like the noonday sun. Psalms 37:5-6, NIV

Commit to the Lord whatever you do, and he will establish your plans. Proverbs 16:3, NIV

"Truly I tell you, if anyone says to this mountain, 'Go, throw yourself into the sea,' and does not doubt in their heart but believes that what they say will happen, it will be done for them." Mark 11:23, NIV

Now faith is confidence in what we hope for and assurance about what we do not see. Hebrews 11:1, NIV

But when you ask, you must believe and not doubt, because the one who doubts is like a wave of the sea, blown and tossed by the wind. James 1:6, NIV

QUESTIONS FOR REFLECTION

1. What part of Gideon's story stood out to me, and why?

_____

_____

_____

2. What has God been calling me to do?

_____

_____

_____

3. What excuses have I spoken over myself that I need to stop saying?

_____

_____

_____

4. In what areas of my life have I allowed doubt to rule over my faith?

_____

_____

_____

PRAYER

After you ask yourself these questions, pray and ask God to deliver you from your doubts:

"Dear God, thank you for being patient with me when I doubt. Thank you for giving me confirmations when I'm too fearful to take steps of faith. Thank you for seeing the end result in me and not my mess. Thank you for loving me and meeting me where I am. Thank you for providing where it seems there isn't provision. Thank you for loving me enough to not leave me in places of complacency. Amen."

CHAPTER 4

God Uses the Broken: Naomi

Ruth 1–4

In the book of Ruth, we learn from Ruth what it truly means to have a servant's heart. It's also a beautiful love story between Ruth and Boaz. Boaz was Ruth's knight in shining armor. However, in this chapter, we aren't going to look at how Ruth did amazingly more than most of us would do considering the situation, and we aren't going to focus on the love story. We are actually going to take a look at a woman named Naomi, Ruth's mother-in-law, who knew what it meant to have a broken heart and be in a season of brokenness.

TOO MUCH TO BEAR

Naomi, her husband, and her sons were from Bethlehem in Judah. They moved to the land of Moab, and her sons married Moabite women: one was named Orpah and the other named Ruth. There in a strange land, Naomi experienced the pain of having her husband pass away and several years later her two sons as well.

Can you imagine? Trying to wrap my mind around what Naomi went through gives me a headache. I can't begin to try to understand her situation. Losing a loved one is so devastating. But losing a husband and both children is entirely too much to bear.

Naomi was feeling radically broken and lost and grew angry and bitter. She even told everyone around her to call her Mara instead of Naomi because it means bitter. She felt as though God had brought misfortune upon her.

Naomi told both of her daughters-in-law to go back to their homes because she couldn't bear any more children for them to marry, which was traditionally what they did in this situation. She wanted to give up completely. She was waving her white flag high in the sky. She was done. She wasn't surrendering to God; she was surrendering to the pain and brokenness. Naomi allowed herself to crawl into a dark hole and stay there for a while.

Yet even in all that brokenness, God was going to use Naomi.

THE CIRCLE OF BLESSING

One of Naomi's daughters-in-law, Ruth, was there for Naomi in her time of hurting and need. She stayed faithfully by Naomi's side. Because of Ruth's obedience to be a blessing to Naomi, God was going to use Naomi to be a blessing to Ruth. Naomi helped Ruth find a husband, and Ruth then started a family, which blessed

Naomi in return. That's how God works: when we choose to be a blessing, we not only get the blessing of being a blessing, but God often blesses us as well.

When Naomi finally got her eyes off of her problems and refocused on God, she was able to be the mom, mentor, and cheerleader that Ruth needed. She helped Ruth find a new husband named Boaz, who was a relative on her husband's side. Boaz took Ruth as his bride, and they had a son named Obed. Naomi took care of Obed like he was her own son. He helped heal her heart. You see, even when Naomi thought her story was over because of the unbearable loss she endured, it was truly only the beginning. Obed grew up and became the father of Jesse, who was the father of David, and that bloodline continued all the way to Jesus.

If only Naomi knew the bloodline of her family would one day include Jesus, I think she would say, "No way! That's amazing! Oh my stars!" Of course, I totally don't know what she would say; however, I think that would be my response if I was her. Plus I'd be doing crazy dance moves such as the grocery cart, the lawn mower, baking the cookies, the sprinkler, and the fish. The list could go on and on. Yes, these are dance moves that I totally rock even though I look like a nerd! But my youth students love it— okay, they like to laugh at it. But anyway, let's get back on track!

When Naomi was in a bottomless pit, feeling so broken and lost, she probably felt unusable. But God used her time of trouble to show others that even when the world seems to be crumbling around you, He can make something beautiful out of something tragic and horrible. The biggest tests of Naomi's life became her biggest testimony of God's faithfulness in the eye of the storm. I bet she didn't know that her struggle-story-turned-beautiful would minister to generations of people and be one of the headlines in the Holy Bible.

God can take our darkest broken moments and make them beautiful mosaic masterpieces.

BENT NOT BROKEN

At the end of the story, we see how Naomi was able to overcome the bitterness and brokenness and, with Ruth's encouragement, reach a place of hope, joy, comfort, peace, and restoration.

No matter what you go through in this life, you have to remember that brokenness is a choice. Yes, I said it. You have the freedom to choose to stay in the pit or find your way out and tell others your story. You can choose to be bent not broken. I have gone through experiences in my life that have completely devastated me to my core, but when I realized that I didn't have to stay in a broken place and could choose to be bent not broken, I finally experienced freedom and peace.

A TALE OF TWO FRIENDS

I have a dear sweet friend named Pam who is one of my prayer partners and like a sister to me. She lost her husband, Bob, two years ago due to a heart attack. They have two boys together. At the time of Bob's passing, one was in middle school, the other high school. It was one of the toughest times I have watched one of my friends go through. Yet, Pam has gone through this hardship with grace and complete faith.

I officiated her husband's funeral, which truth be told was extremely hard for me because my heart ached and broke for her and her boys. Every time I would make eye contact with them during Bob's service, I got a huge lump in my throat and just wanted to hold them and cry with them.

Since Bob died, Pam has had to step into the role as mom AND dad. She went from having a husband to rely on to being the sole provider for her family. She has handled the day-to-day frustrations with the house, with finances, and with having two teenage boys, which—let's be honest—is a FULL task in itself!

Pam told me at one point she felt as though she was playing a whack-a-mole game in life. After Bob died, it was one obstacle after another. One problem would be solved, and then just like whack-a-mole, another one would arise. As she would tell me what was going on, I would sit in amazement that she was still able to have a smile on her face and make jokes, even laugh.

Once she had squirrels get in her attic, and instead of calling a pest control company to help move her new furry friends, Pam decided to get a cage and handle it herself to save money. She got the squirrels out of her attic safe and sound by putting peanut butter in the cage and relocating them to a place where they could roam freely without destroying her house.

She has had to pull up carpet herself because her house flooded. She even repaired a hole with tools that she never thought she would be able to use, let alone be able to identify. She makes jokes about the carpet and the hole being shabby chic.

With all of this drama going on, she is a teacher's assistant helping children with special needs, has faithfully served in youth ministry working with inner city students, sings on the praise team at church, and is also starting to pursue the call of being a Christian women's speaker and author. She found this new strength that she didn't even know she had and went skydiving and wants to go again.

Wow. Wow. Wow. I still sit in amazement of Pam's story of faithfulness and trust in the Lord. Instead of playing the blame game, wasting time, and running away from the Lord, she ran toward God and let Him use her in her brokenness. It is very, very evident that God is the only One carrying Pam and giving her supernatural strength and peace. I know God will bring her another husband someday to love her and her boys.

Annette is also a best friend who is like a sister and a prayer partner who has served alongside me in ministry for many years. She lost her husband, Rudy, due to cancer eleven years ago. Annette's testimony is very powerful and aligns with what I call the "Naomi approach." Much like Naomi, she was bitter, hopeless, and angry at the loss of her best friend and husband. Annette allowed bitterness to dictate her life for a season. She didn't understand why God would give her a husband she loved and adored only to take him away from her.

She ran from God and found herself entangled with bad influences and entrapped in relational temptations. The shackles of sin seemed so great, but Satan is on a leash and God is holding the leash. As she tells people, God pursued her and never gave up on her, even though she proclaimed to have given up on Him. He used the choices she made during that broken and dark time to make Annette the amazing woman she is today. She gets so excited when she talks about the goodness and faithfulness of God in her own life.

Looking at Annette now, you would never know that this woman was once at odds with God. At her job, people know her as a devoted follower of Jesus and that's because the love of Jesus oozes out of her: it's contagious. She also serves at her church and at a non-profit ministry that helps people overcome addiction and struggles with sex and relationships. She is a leader everywhere she goes and truly a force to be reckoned with. I've watched her overcome obstacles over the years; she went through breast cancer and came out stronger than she was before. Passionate about her faith in God, she is constantly in God's word, and I'm always amazed at the nuggets of truth that flow freely from her. Honestly, I feel like I should follow her around with a notebook as she talks. Those nuggets are pure gold! Annette's story is parallel to Naomi's in many ways because they both went from being bitter and broken to joyful and healed.

Two of my best friends have walked through a loss similar to Naomi. They both handled it differently, but the result is the same: they are now passionate about their Heavenly Father. They took their mess and made it their message. They took the hurt and pain and turned it into joy and peace.

You have the power to do the same thing. I don't know where you are at or what you are going through right now in your life. But I do know it isn't a coincidence that you picked up this book and began reading it. I know in my heart because I am praying right now that whoever reads this book will be blessed and healed. Maybe you can relate to Naomi's story, Pam's story, or Annette's story. I pray that you have peace knowing that you are not the only one who has endured the pain of loss and feeling completely broken.

Your story isn't over.

BIG CHRIS

I am currently a youth pastor at a church where I work with inner city students. They are absolutely amazing in every way—I love them so much! They have overcome abandonment, separation from family members in jail, gang involvement, drug use, abuse in all forms, and so much more. Each year we take our students to camp but have to partner with other churches to make it happen. Unfortunately, not many churches are willing to partner with us because our students come from such rough backgrounds.

However, Chris welcomed us with open arms. Chris was also a youth pastor. He was known as "Big Chris," this teddy bear, larger-than-life man who would always raise his big paws up high during worship. He was extremely funny and loved goofing around with students. Every student, and especially my students, were drawn to Chris. He understood them because he had experienced similar struggles in his own life.

We used to joke around because my youth group consisted of mostly boys and Chris's youth group consisted of mostly girls, and one of Chris's volunteers said at camp that I had the youth group Chris always wanted and he had the youth group I always wanted. We all had a laugh knowing good and well that it was only half true because we loved where God had strategically put us.

Chris opened up to some of my students about the hardships he had growing up. I always appreciated how he would seek them out to share how God got a hold of him and totally transformed him, putting him in a much better place than when he was without Jesus. They could see Jesus in Chris. Isn't it amazing how God can use our brokenness to relate to others and help them?

I didn't know that last year at camp would be the last time we would see Big Chris. He died suddenly and unexpectedly due to a horrible seizure. Everyone was left feeling completely lost and devastated, especially his beautiful wife Christina and two daughters.

At Chris's funeral, when the family came in and everyone was standing up out of respect for them, a familiar voice was heard all throughout the church. It was Chris's deep, raspy voice. He started telling everyone there how he came to be known as "Big Chris." They were playing a recording of him giving his testimony at church! When the family sat down, we all sat down and stared at this empty pulpit as Chris shared with us his passion for Jesus his Savior. Even though Chris wasn't physically there, he was still preaching about God's faithfulness at his own funeral!

That's how God works: He can use the absolute worst circumstances and make a beautiful picture out of it, just like He did for Naomi, Pam, Annette, and Chris's wife, Christina. I hope and pray that when it's my time to go and be with the Lord that I can leave a mark like Chris did.

Not long ago, his beautiful wife, Christina, found a notebook of Chris's and shared on Facebook what he wrote. After reading it, I knew it was perfect for this book. Here's what Chris wrote: "God can use anyone to help him in His work. We shouldn't feel unqualified because of our appearance, lack of education, or our past. We should always remember that the highest calling in life is serving God, no matter what the world or friends may say. Money, popularity, and power can't compare to a relationship with Christ." I bet Chris had no idea that his quote in a random notebook would actually become a powerful quote in a book.

Wow. Wow. Wow. Yep, I totally said it again, and expect me to say it a few more times as we go through this book. Chris understood something that most people unfortunately don't even figure out during their lifetime. He understood the simple truth of it all. Having a relationship with Christ is everything.

BEAUTY IN THE BROKENNESS

I will never understand why Chris had to pass away when he did. I will never understand why Rudy had to pass away when he did. I will never understand why Bob had to pass away when he did. I honestly can't even fathom what Naomi had to go through when she lost her husband and two sons, but I do understand that God says we have but one appointed time to die: "There is a time for everything, and a season for every activity under the heavens: a time to be born and a time to die" (Ecclesiastes 3:1–2a, NIV). God's ways are higher, and his thoughts are higher. God's plans are always bigger and often different than our own.

I chose to share the stories of Naomi, Pam, Annette, and Big Chris to show you that even in the most unexpected and hurtful situations when we feel completely devastated and broken, we need to remember that GOD IS FAITHFUL! He can and does use all situations for our good. He is faithful even when we don't understand why things happen the way that they do.

In His greatness, He takes our biggest pains—the times where we are left feeling broken and devastated and we have no strength left—and He creates beauty, wholeness, peace, and trust. When we don't have any control over the situation at hand and all we have left is to trust God, that's when the beauty of brokenness outshines the darkness. It's a beautiful mess watching things fall apart only to fall together stronger and better than before. It's only God's hand that is capable of such a thing.

Much like God pressing on Naomi's heart to help Ruth find a husband, God has asked me to do several things that I didn't fully understand. He may ask you to do something that doesn't make sense to you at the time:

To go pray with someone you don't know.

To give an encouraging word to a stranger.

To pay for someone's coffee or food in the drive-thru line.

To volunteer your time to help someone in need.

To help someone, which might mean putting yourself and your plans on pause.

But I have found that when I listened to God, there was blessing on the other side of the obedience. Don't delay; go obey. Don't rob others of their blessing, and don't rob yourself from being a blessing.

There are always blessings on the other side of obedience. When Naomi put her own emotions on pause and was obedient to help Ruth in an impossible time of grief, there was blessing for Naomi and Ruth on the other side. When Pam, Annette, and Christina held on to God's peace during their time of loss, there were blessings in the mess. Don't quit before reaching the blessing. God doesn't want you to miss out. But God gives you the freedom to choose. The question is, what will you choose?

FOCUS VERSES

Those who know your name trust in you, for you, Lord, have never forsaken those who seek you. Psalm 9:10, NIV

The Lord is close to the brokenhearted and saves those who are crushed in spirit. Psalms 34:18, NIV

I will say of the Lord, "He is my refuge and my fortress, my God, in whom I trust." Psalm 91:2, NIV

Trust in the Lord with all your heart and lean not on your own understanding; in all your ways submit to him, and he will make your paths straight. Proverbs 3:5–6, NIV

"Surely God is my salvation; I will trust and not be afraid. The Lord, the Lord himself, is my strength and my defense; he has become my salvation." Isaiah 12:2, NIV

You will keep in perfect peace those whose minds are steadfast, because they trust in you. Isaiah 26:3, NIV

QUESTIONS FOR REFLECTION

1. How do I relate to Naomi's story?

_____

_____

_____

2. How do I relate to these stories of brokenness?

_____

_____

_____

3. What broken places in my life do I need to surrender to God?

_____

_____

_____

4. How can I use the brokenness in my life to help others?

_____

_____

_____

PRAYER

After you ask yourself these questions, pray and ask God to deliver you from brokenness:

"Dear God, these places of brokenness in my life need healing. Help me remember that I may be bent but I'm not broken. Help me, God, to forgive others who may have caused me to feel broken. Help me have the strength to overcome any obstacles that I am facing and any obstacles that come my way. You, God, are my strength. You are my everything. Help me remember that you are with me. Help me remember that you, God, will never leave me. Amen."

CHAPTER 5
God Uses the Sinful: David

2 Samuel 11

Everywhere you look there are tabloids exposing people's wrongs, shortcomings, or—as God calls them—sins. It's really sad how sin means money, so it's highlighted in the news. The greatest news story of all time happened over 2,000 years ago when Jesus Christ was born and at 33 years old died and defeated sin and death forever. Jesus had a three-year ministry that would forever change history. That's what they really should be talking and writing about. The good news of Jesus Christ should not only get people excited, but it should also put a fire in their spirit. But, unfortunately, sin sells. People chase after sin because it looks so appealing and free, when in reality all it does is lead them into a trap that they can't escape without Jesus.

In this broken world, if you aren't happy with your spouse or significant other, it's considered an acceptable choice to just go get someone else who meets your needs, even if that someone else already belongs to someone else. In this chapter, we are going to look at a sinful man who was not only an adulterer but a murderer, too. Yet God says that this sinful man had a heart after His heart: "But God removed Saul and replaced him with David, a man about whom God said, 'I have found David son of Jesse, a man after my own heart. He will do everything I want him to do' " (Acts 13:22, NLT).

WRAPPED UP IN SIN

In Psalms, you see many poems, prayers, and praises that David wrote about the strength, power, and faithfulness of his God. He knew that God was the One who enabled him to defeat bears, lions, and Goliath. God was the One who helped David outsmart and outrun King Saul when he wanted to kill David. God helped David become king and protected David when his enemies were ready to kill him. And God loved David in spite of his weakness and shortcomings.

One evening David went out on the roof of his palace and was walking around. From the rooftop, he spotted a beautiful woman bathing. Her name was Bathsheba. When David saw her, he lustfully wanted her and pursued her. He ordered his messengers to get her and bring her to the palace. When she was brought to the palace, David and Bathsheba slept together and she became pregnant.

From that point on, David was so wrapped up in his sin that he tried to cover it up by taking Bathsheba's husband Uriah completely out of the picture. Uriah was a soldier in David's army. David conspired to put Uriah on the front lines of his army to ensure that he would die. David's plan worked. He killed off Bathsheba's husband, but it came with an unbearable price, as sin always does. David and Bathsheba's son who was conceived during their affair ended up getting sick and dying.

When David realized that he had sinned against the Lord, he genuinely asked for God's forgiveness. God is a merciful and forgiving God. All we have to do is simply ask Him to forgive us and He always does. David knew the choices he had made weren't the best and definitely weren't God's best for him. However, God saw past the sin, examined David's heart, and found that he was repentant. And God forgave him.

God not only forgave him, but He also continued to use David and bless him. God gave David and Bathsheba another son, and they named him Solomon. David remained king for the rest of his days and led the Israelites to victory in many battles. David didn't allow himself to stay focused on his shortcomings; he understood the importance of focusing on the blessings along the way.

BLUEPRINTS FOR OVERCOMING SIN

In one of my favorite bible stories, sin is put in its place. Matthew 4:1–10 is the story of Jesus being tempted after He was baptized in the Jordan River. Led by the Holy Spirit, He fasted for forty days in the desert. After the forty days were over, Jesus was, of course, hungry and tired. That's when the devil loves to come and mislead us into sin. He tries to break us when we are on the verge of breaking. Jesus went through and passed three tests from the devil.

First, the devil tried to tempt Jesus to use His supernatural powers for His own benefit instead of relying on God to satisfy His hunger. In the second test, the devil tried to tempt Jesus to test God by acting selfishly and seeing if God would intervene. The third test was a temptation for power. The devil was trying to offer Jesus everything He already had. Jesus had and always has had authority, power, and much more than this world could ever offer.

The Bible gives us this story of Jesus as one of many blueprints for overcoming sin in our lives. It shows how the enemy is very predictable and isn't very creative. But he's very much alive and on a mission to take us out: "Be alert and of sober mind. Your enemy the devil prowls around like a roaring lion looking for someone to devour" (1 Peter 5:8, NIV).

The evil one and his evil schemes will try to trip us up. To stand our ground, we need to "put on the full armor of God" daily (Ephesians 6:13). The sword of the Spirit is God's word. Unfortunately, the majority of Christians aren't reading God's word; therefore, they might be dressed for battle, but they don't have a weapon to fight with. The Bible is God's love letter to us to equip us in all situations. All throughout the Bible, God lays out people's lives as additional blueprints for what to do and what not to do so that we can know how to handle life and how to beat the enemy. Since we are sinful creatures, we can't afford to forget our armor, especially God's word!

We have all the tools to overcome sin through God's word and the Holy Spirit. But we have the freedom to ignore God's word and the Holy Spirit and take a rougher route that God doesn't intend for us. When we choose the rough route, God can use our messes to make a beautiful picture in our lives that will keep others from repeating our mistakes and help them overcome. He is so creative that way!

GOD > SATAN

You have a target on your back that says "God's Child," and it makes the enemy angry. The evil one doesn't want you to flourish, and he definitely doesn't want you to fulfill your God-given purpose. Believe me, the last thing that he wants is for you to accomplish God's best in your life. I have allowed the enemy to keep me from writing this book now for nine years. But not any longer! Rest assured, our God is bigger and stronger than the enemy.

People have this misconception that Satan has equal power with God, but he doesn't. No one, nothing, can even remotely come close to God. You have a Heavenly Father who knows His purpose for you and even called you by name before you were even conceived, who walks in front of you, beside you, and behind you; who is cheering you on; and who is wanting you to succeed! God cares about you so much that He even knows how many hairs are on your head. He also knows the deepest, darkest sins that you have committed or ever will commit, yet HE STILL LOVES YOU, HE STILL WANTS YOU, and HE HASN'T GIVEN UP ON YOU. God has wonderful plans for you: "'For I know the plans I have for you,' declares the Lord, 'plans to prosper you and not to harm you, plans to give you hope and a future. Then you will call on me and come and pray to me, and I will listen to you'" (Jeremiah 29:11-12, NIV). But you have to choose it. You can choose to walk away from whatever is keeping you in bondage. You have the free will to do so.

YOUR CHOICE

Understand this, God gives us free will. As He did with David, He allows us to choose the direction we go with our lives. We get to determine how rough or how smooth our journey will be. No matter what we choose, God can still get us where He wants us to go because His plans always prevail. When we are tempted and we choose to sin and take the rough route, God always provides a way out of sin so we can get back on the right track. We just simply have to choose God's way instead of our sinful ways. It's not easy, but it's not impossible, either. Even if we choose God's way, we will still go through rough patches because this world is broken, but the hard times will be far less painful with God than without Him.

Only you and God know your deepest struggles with sin. If you know that you have eyes that tend to wander, then don't allow yourself to be put in situations where your eyes wander. Obviously, you can't control what people look like or what other people wear when you at the grocery store, running errands, or even at church. But you can choose to look or to look away.

I've always loved and appreciated how my husband, Matt, immediately stares into my eyes if we encounter a woman who isn't dressed modestly—even if she is on television or in a movie. It has always made me feel so validated and comforted to know that my husband intentionally chooses to look away when given the opportunity to be tempted.

AN OFFER OF FORGIVENESS

The story of the woman at the well truly coincides with David's story and is another story that I love. In John 4, we see Jesus reach out to someone who was an "outsider" to the people in the town of Sychar in Samaria because of her sinful choices. She was known as the town harlot.

She went to get water at the well when no one else was around to avoid the condemnation and ridicule of the people's gossip and assumptions about her. She got caught off guard when Jesus sought her out and asked her to give him a drink of water. Mind you, she wasn't only the town harlot, but she was a Samaritan and Jews like Jesus normally didn't associate with Samaritans. But Jesus being Jesus didn't care about what everyone else was doing or what they thought. Jesus reached out to the woman who was "unusable" in everyone's eyes. He offered her living water so that she wouldn't ever thirst again. Jesus is the living water; with Him, your soul will never run dry. Jesus offered her forgiveness and told her that she was worthy and able regardless of her past choices.

Like the woman at the well, maybe you're tired of always taking the rough route that God didn't intend for you. Maybe you're tired of doing the same thing again and again and getting the same or worse results, which is insanity. Don't just give up and lay there in your brokenness feeling hopeless. You need to get back up. Just ask God for forgiveness, and start making the changes that you need to make to get back on track.

GRACE UNDESERVED

I thank God every day for giving me an amazing earthly father and mother. They taught me about Jesus. They showed me what it means to live for God by being leaders at church, giving cheerfully, and encouraging and helping others with a servant's heart. In my teen years, I was making choices that weren't the best. My parents met me where I was at and loved me, even if that place wasn't a great one. On one specific occasion, I came to tell them my mess, and instead of disowning me or throwing me out, they embraced me.

I was only fourteen years old, and I thought I was pregnant.

I remember confiding in my small group leader at youth. I didn't know how I was going to tell my parents. She told me that she would be there for me if I needed her. But because she knew my parents, she knew I would be okay.

Sure enough, when I talked to my parents about my situation, my mom held me and cried with me. In a calm, steady voice, my dad said, "Well, Carri, we love you like God loves you so know that we will get through this together." My mom and dad showed me the love and grace of God. They gave it to me even when I didn't deserve it. Their response grabbed ahold of my heart and, for the first time, opened my eyes to the meaning of undeserved grace. Growing up, I had heard the story of God's love and Christ's sacrifice for our sins, but I had never encountered forgiveness on such a level. The situation helped me grasp what our Heavenly Father did for us. My parents made it easier for me to understand my need for God and the love I have for Him.

Several other times in my life I have chosen to sin instead of clinging to God's truth. Who am I kidding? It hasn't been several times in my life, but several times DAILY. More times than I can count, I have gone in the opposite direction than where God intended for me to go. For so long, I've allowed my sins to dictate and paralyze every single move I make. I've allowed my sins to put labels on me that God doesn't even see anymore because of Jesus and my repentant heart. I even used my sins as a crutch to excuse why I wasn't able or capable. If you allow your sins to trap you in a mindset of being unusable, then you are only robbing yourself and others of the blessings that God wants to do in you and through you.

When sin entraps us and we feel like our world is collapsing around us, we never realize that God could actually use our mistakes to help others. For me, it has truly been a blessing to be able to help teens and their families when they are faced with similar situations. Because I have also gone through it, they know that they are not alone. If this is you, know that you are not alone. There is hope. Just hold on, God has you and He won't ever let go.

ARMS OPEN WIDE

Maybe as you're reading this chapter, you have conviction in your heart. Can I encourage you that it's all right? It's okay that you messed up; it's not the end of the world. Truth is, we ALL mess up. Remember, David committed adultery, told lies, and had someone murdered!

No matter how serious, God can transform any situation. There isn't anything too big for God to handle, and not only handle, but heal. In ministry, I've seen Him at work. I've seen situations of adultery be turned into a testimony of forgiveness. I've seen men and women addicted to pornography healed and whole. I've seen women and men break the lie of the evil one telling them it's okay to sleep around and give themselves away to people. I've seen students who come from abusive homes come out being loud and bold voices against abuse. God is the perfect healer in any and all situations.

Whatever your situation is, please know that God will meet you where you are. He loves you right where you are. And, like David, He will forgive you, continue to use you, and bless you.

Jesus came and died for you, and His arms were spread out wide to forgive all the sins of this broken world, which includes your sins and mine. Jesus was the perfect sacrifice. He defeated death and sin forever. He has forgiven us.

So let go of your past. Don't allow yourself to be in bondage anymore. He has freed us. Believe me, God's shoulders are stronger than anyone's, and Jesus wants to embrace you regardless of your past history. He wants to help you write your future. All you have to do is allow Him to do so. So why wait any longer? Stop pushing God out of your way. Ask Him to guide you, help you, and heal you, and I promise you won't regret it.

FOCUS VERSES

Above all else, guard your heart, for everything you do flows from it. Proverbs 4:23, NIV

No temptation has overtaken you except what is common to mankind. And God is faithful; he will not let you be tempted beyond what you can bear. But when you are tempted, he will also provide a way out so you can endure it. 1 Corinthians 9:13, NIV

For I can do everything through Christ, who gives me strength. Philippians 4:13, NLT

If we confess our sins, he is faithful and just and will forgive us our sins and purify us from all unrighteousness. 1 John 1:9, NIV

QUESTIONS FOR REFLECTION

1. How do I relate to David's story?

_____

_____

_____

2. Are my choices causing me to take the rough route or the route God intended me to take? How can I get back on the right track?

_____

3. What do I need to let go of so that I can get back on track?

_____

_____

_____

4. How can I use my shortcomings to help others?

_____

_____

_____

PRAYER

After you ask yourself these questions, pray and ask God to deliver you from your sins:

"Dear God, thank you for forgiving the inexcusable in me. Help me remember to forgive the inexcusable in others who have hurt me. Help me remember that my past doesn't define me. Remind me, Lord, that you have forgiven me, and I don't have to be in bondage anymore. Amen."

CHAPTER 6

God Uses the Unwilling: Jonah

Jonah 1–4

Jonah is one of those bible stories that we are taught in children's
church, and then we don't really think about it much anymore. But
I think we are missing out on some good lessons with the story of
Jonah. God called Jonah to preach to the people of Nineveh to stop
their wicked ways. Jonah didn't want this job at all, so he chose to
ignore the call and run away from it. He had an unwilling heart.

WARNING: DETOUR AHEAD!

Since Jonah was ignoring the call and avoiding his mission, he
chose to get on a boat and literally go in the opposite geographical
direction of his call. He was planning to go to Tarshish when God
was calling him to Nineveh. It breaks my heart when some people
hear the truth and know the truth, but when push comes to shove,
they still choose to ignore God completely.

As Jonah was traveling to Tarshish, a huge storm came. The ship was about to break into pieces, and the sailors on board were frantically trying to figure out why this was all happening. They were terrified and were calling out in desperation to their gods, but their gods didn't answer. They even threw all the non-essentials overboard to try to lighten the load of the ship.

Meanwhile, Jonah was asleep, so the captain came and woke him up and told him to pray to his God. The sailors all decided to draw straws, and they claimed that whoever had the shortest straw was the culprit for all of this. Guess who drew the shortest straw? Yep! It was Jonah! God has an amazing sense of humor! This sounds like a scene out of a comedy movie!

After getting the shortest straw, Jonah ended up telling the men his story, and they all realized that Jonah was running away from God. Jonah told them that the only way to stop the storm was to throw him overboard. They didn't want to do what he said at first, but the storm grew stronger so they threw Jonah overboard. When Jonah hit the sea, the storm finally stopped. Recognizing the power of Jonah's God, the men started praising Him and devoted themselves to Him. Clearly, Jonah's God was the one true God.

Isn't God amazing? Even when we take a wrong turn or a detour and when we aren't willing, God doesn't waste any of it. Jonah had the opportunity to witness to these men, and they came to know the one true God.

After Jonah was thrown into the sea and the storm stopped, God sent a big fish to swallow Jonah. Now, I know what you're thinking: WHY? Well, if God didn't send the fish, Jonah would have drowned. I think sometimes when we attempt to make detours in God's plan, God allows the detours to refine us, but then He saves us and brings us back to His plans for us.

A LITTLE TIME-OUT

Jonah was in the belly of a fish for three days and three nights. I don't know about you, but I'd be FREAKING OUT! Talk about claustrophobic! Basically, Jonah had to take a time-out to think about everything. Yes, like a good Father, God gave Jonah a time-out. God gave me a time-out once, okay, a few times, and each time wasn't fun, but I definitely learned my lesson.

In the belly of the fish, Jonah was able to get clarity. He started thanking God for saving him from drowning. He told God that he would do what he was supposed to do, and he would praise God as he was doing it. God spoke to the fish, and the fish vomited Jonah up on the seashore. Ewww, can you imagine what Jonah must have looked and smelled like? #nasty #showerimmediately

GOD WINS

But God didn't just make the fish vomit Jonah up on any seashore: He had the fish deliver Jonah to the call! Jonah was in Nineveh. See, I told you, God wins every time!

Nineveh was a huge city, so it took Jonah three days to walk across it. Jonah then started preaching to the people of Nineveh, telling them what had happened to him and that if they didn't change their wicked ways God would destroy their city in forty days. The people listened to Jonah and repented. God saw this change of heart, and in His loving grace, He decided not to destroy the city because the people were truly repentant.

A TEMPER TANTRUM

Now you would think that Jonah would see all of this unfold and be happy. The people changed, God forgave them, and all was right with the world. However, Jonah was not feeling happy at all:

> Jonah was furious. He lost his temper. He yelled at God, "God! I knew it—when I was back home, I knew this was going to happen! That's why I ran off to Tarshish! I knew you were sheer grace and mercy, not easily angered, rich in love, and ready at the drop of a hat to turn your plans of punishment into a program of forgiveness!" (Jonah 4:1–2, MSG)

Okay, so after reading those verses, I can totally see one of my children having a similar tantrum. Maybe I've even thrown a tantrum like this one to God. Like I told you, I'm not perfect. Jonah was having a tantrum because he knew God was going to forgive the people, and he didn't think they deserved it. He forgot that God forgave him for running away from his mission in the first place! Isn't that what we do? We want the unforgivable to be forgiven in us, but we don't want to forgive the unforgivable in someone else.

LIFE LESSONS

Now God is a good, good, Father to us. He won't allow us to be stagnant, and He won't allow us to be complacent in our lives. God is also a good teacher. At the end of the book of Jonah, He taught Jonah an amazing object lesson. Jonah went off and started to sulk all by himself because he didn't like how everything turned out. I'm sure you haven't done anything like that before. I know I haven't. #yeahrightcarri #Ivedoneitmorethanonce

As Jonah was busy feeling sorry for himself and angry at God's grace, he put together a shelter of leafy branches and sat there in the shade to see what would happen to the city of Nineveh. God arranged for a tree to spring up to provide Jonah shade. The shade tree got Jonah out of his angry sulk, and it cooled him off, too. God then sent a worm to destroy the shade tree. Jonah became furious. He even prayed to die because he was so mad at his situation. I love what God said to Jonah:

> "What right do you have to get angry about this shade tree?"
>
> Jonah said, "Plenty of right. It's made me angry enough to die!"
>
> God said, "What's this? How is it that you can change your feelings from pleasure to anger overnight about a

mere shade tree that you did nothing to get? You neither planted nor watered it. It grew up one night and died the next night. So why can't I likewise change what I feel about Nineveh from anger to pleasure, this big city of more than 120,000 childlike people who don't yet know right from wrong, to say nothing of all the innocent animals?" (Jonah 4:9–11, MSG)

I love how God always makes teachable moments. God was giving Jonah an unforgettable life lesson. God was trying to show Jonah that just as Jonah's mind changed, God can change His mind, too.

God is a good Teacher and Father who wants to see His children succeed. He wants His kids to flourish in all that they do. He gives us the freedom to choose. He also gives us many, many chances to choose Him and His perfect will for us. God doesn't give up on us, even when we are unwilling to obey Him or do what He asks us to do.

LEARNING TO LISTEN TO GOD

Many times in my life, I have chosen to go in the opposite direction of God's plans because I was scared and didn't believe. For example, when I felt God telling me to write this book, I kept putting it off. I listened to the self-talk of doubt and fear and constantly made excuses for why I couldn't write a book. I even told God that I hated to read, so why would He have me write a book?

For so long, I was an expert in making excuses for why I couldn't and why I wasn't capable. That's not what God wants for us, though. He wants us to understand fully that we are equipped. We are anointed and appointed for such a time as this. God literally has a geographical location for each of us to dominate for His namesake. God will send divine appointments in your life to steer you in the right direction. If you open your heart to listen, God's voice becomes magnified everywhere you are. He can use anything and anyone to get our attention.

I believe that God speaks to each of His children uniquely because each of us are different and unique. Many times I have had encounters that I know only came from God. I have been driving down the street and crying out to God to give me a word, and then I have driven past a billboard that says something I needed to hear. I have been in my car praying and a song has come on the radio that spurs me on to keep going forward. I have even gone to the store, thinking that I wouldn't see anyone and, of course, looking like a hot mess. But I'm thankful that Jesus loves this hot mess! I always run into someone there at the store who reminds me of my purpose, my mission. God even speaks to me through movies and television shows.

When I finally got to a place where I sincerely wanted to listen to God and the mission He had for me, everything started coming together in a beautiful way.

THE STRUGGLE IS REAL

Sometimes we are unwilling because it doesn't make any logical sense to go ahead and do what we feel God wants us to do. We have this inner struggle between our mind and our spirit. I know that, for myself, I delayed the mission I felt God calling me to because it didn't make sense to me. I also felt like I had to apologize for doing what I felt God was calling me to do, which was completely the enemy trying to detour me from my mission. The enemy isn't creative; he's strategic. He will often use the people and things most precious to you to be the very things that hold you back from obedience.

I bet you have encountered the same thing in your life. What we have to understand is that our calling probably won't make sense to someone who doesn't have a similar calling, gifting, or passion. I can't tell you how many times I have tried to talk with people in my life about what I felt God was asking me to do, and they looked at me like I had gone absolutely bonkers. On my vision board, I had dreams displayed that people didn't think I could ever make come true. But if God's in it, it flows; if He's not in it, it's forced. Nothing and no one can stop what God has already destined for you.

I was also told that I needed to just focus on one thing at a time. But my brain doesn't work that way. I constantly have to be doing something or creating something—that's how God made me. For so long, I felt as though I was weird for having a desire to pursue all that I felt God calling me to do. I'm sure other people thought to themselves, "What is she doing now?" I allowed others to speak over me who were too afraid to go toward what God had called them to do. You always need to make sure that you consider the source attempting to speak into your life. If they tell you something and aren't walking with the Lord, then take it with a grain of salt. If they are walking with the Lord, take it to the Lord and let Him give you confirmation. If it's not from Him, He will make it clear to you.

THE BEAUTY OF OBEDIENCE

I love to encourage people to use the gifts and talents that God has given them. I love watching people trust God and do what they are supposed to do, what they were made to do. One of my sweet friends, Megan, just started a podcast called *A Mom's Story*. It's a podcast of different moms and their stories of inspiration and encouragement. Megan has had this podcast on her heart for some time now. She finally decided to step out in faith and be obedient to do what God asked her to do.

The other day Megan interviewed me on her podcast, and we had an absolute blast together. I was so excited and proud to see Megan use her gifting and creativity as she was interviewing me. She made interviewing look effortless. She kept doing things on her computer, and for someone who is tech-challenged, I was so impressed! The beauty of obedience is overwhelming, especially when it has a ripple effect and spurs others on to step out in faith to do their own mission that God has designed for them. It's so powerful!

NOT ALLOWED TO STAY

God met Jonah in his hot mess, just like He meets us in our hot mess. He gave Jonah a ministry even when his attitude wasn't always the best. In His faithfulness, He brought Jonah back to where He called him to go. He met Jonah in the mess but didn't and wouldn't let him stay there. God won't let you or me stay there, either. He helped Jonah get out of his broken way of thinking and gave him clarity. God loves us too much to allow us to stay in broken places; He has something for us to do. Just like loving parents want the very best for their kids, God wants the absolute best for us!

It may be for days, months, or even years that you have been unwilling to do something that you know God has put on your heart and asked you to do. You know I can relate! You can never outrun God. You can't hide from Him. You can't outsmart Him. He will win every single time. I guarantee it! So stop allowing people's opinions and doubts to hold you back. Step out and simply be willing to be used by God to do amazing things!

FOCUS VERSES

You, Lord, are forgiving and good, abounding in love to all who call to you. Psalm 86:5, NIV

In their hearts humans plan their course, but the Lord establishes their steps. Proverbs 16:9, NIV

To do what is right and just is more acceptable to the Lord than sacrifice. Proverbs 21:3, NIV

Many are the plans in a person's heart, but it is the Lord's purpose that prevails. Proverbs 19:21, NIV

QUESTIONS FOR REFLECTION

1. How do I relate to Jonah's story?

_____

_____

_____

2. What am I mad at God about right now?

_____

_____

_____

3. What has God been trying to get my attention about?

_____

_____

_____

4. What divine appointments has God given me lately?

_____

_____

_____

PRAYER

After you ask yourself these questions, pray and ask God to deliver you from your unwillingness:

"Dear God, help me see with your eyes. Help me love with your heart. Don't allow me to be stagnant. Grow me. Pour into me. Help me be the woman or man you have called me to be. I want to go to where you call me. Take me where you want me to go, Father. I want to be obedient. Don't allow me to believe the enemy's lies that say I am unable. With you, God, I know I can. I want to please you, Lord, with my life. Amen."

CHAPTER 7
God Uses the Fearful: Peter

Matthew 14:22–36 and 26:69–75 and John 21:15–23

Peter is one of my favorite people in the Bible because he was the emotional disciple. He was in tune with his emotions and was very vocal about how he felt. Peter was always one of the first ones who had something to say or do, right or wrong. Sometimes his emotions would get the best of him; sometimes his foot ended up in his mouth. But nonetheless, he was very close to Jesus and had good intentions. At the beginning of his journey, he was often fearful and afraid, but God used Peter in mighty ways.

WHO YA GONNA CALL?

I absolutely love the story of Jesus calling Peter to walk on water. After Jesus fed five thousand people with just two fish and five loaves of bread, Jesus told the disciples to get in a boat and go ahead of Him to the next town. The disciples were a good distance away from shore when Jesus decided to walk on the water to get to the boat. When the disciples saw a person on the water, they all started freaking out. Their reaction is humorous to me because they immediately started guessing who it was on the water. Some of them even wondered if it was a ghost. No, you don't need to call Ghostbusters! Hello! Duh! It's obviously Jesus!

Lord knows, I've tried to walk on water several times at my parent's pool, but every single time I immediately sink. You might think I'm kidding, but no, I've actually tried it!

It was dark and the waves were crashing around them. All the disciples except one were unwilling to leave the safety of the boat, though you couldn't be safer than when you're with Jesus! However, Peter shouted to Jesus, "Lord, if it's you, call me and I will come!" So Jesus told Peter to come. Without hesitation, Peter stepped out of the boat in obedience. When his gaze was on Jesus, he was able to do the impossible and walk on water. When Peter took his eyes off of Jesus and onto the waves, he grew afraid and started to sink.

We do that don't we? We allow the waves and distractions of this life to pull our focus, causing us to be fearful and afraid. It also makes us fall short of the blessings God wants for us. We sink into our fears.

I see an example of God's faithfulness when the Bible says that Jesus IMMEDIATELY caught Peter. God loves us and cares deeply for us. Even when we are afraid, God always draws near to us and will catch us when we fall.

I admire the fact that Peter had the guts to step out in faith. Even though the rest of the disciples didn't do it, he did. I want a faith like that. When God calls me to come, I hope and pray that I'll come without hesitation and jump in with both feet. But I know that even in my weakness, God is patient and catches me when my eyes turn away from Him.

THE HULK

Jesus told all of His disciples that He would have to suffer. When Peter protested, "Jesus turned and said to Peter, 'Get behind me, Satan! You are a stumbling block to me; you do not have in mind the concerns of God, but merely human concerns' " (Matthew 16:23, NIV).

I guess the lesson didn't sink in because at the time of Jesus' arrest, Peter was afraid for Jesus and wasn't going to allow them to take Him away without a fight. In John 18:10, the Bible says Peter was the disciple who literally cut off the ear of the chief priest's servant when a mob was trying to take Jesus away to be tried and crucified.

If you think that the Hulk has anger issues, look at Peter!

No matter how hard he tried, Peter could not stop God's plan. Jesus was going to die for us, to defeat sin and death forever.

ROCK ON

It's interesting because even though Jesus called Peter "The Rock"—long before Dwayne "The Rock" Johnson came around—Peter would also be the disciple who denied Jesus! The same night that Jesus was arrested, Peter would deny Jesus three times before the rooster crowed the next morning. Jesus predicted it would happen, but Peter didn't believe that allegation. He never thought that he would be capable of denying Jesus because he loved Jesus so very much. But as Jesus was going through everything leading up to His crucifixion, Peter was afraid and did, in fact, betray Jesus by denying that he knew Jesus three times before he heard a rooster crow.

That rooster crow must have been hard for Peter, maybe even a little crippling. I know that reminders of my mistakes, especially the ones that were crippling, can bring me to my knees. Peter could have allowed his mistakes to dictate his every move and the future of his ministry. He could have decided to wallow in his shame, but he didn't choose to stay in that place. He didn't allow it to hold him back from serving and being a bold voice for the Lord. He was the disciple everyone looked to after Jesus was crucified. The disciples all turned to ask Peter what he thought about everything that had happened. Peter finally became "The Rock."

Peter had a powerful encounter with the resurrected Jesus. Peter talked with Jesus, and Jesus asked Peter three different times if Peter loved Him. All three times Peter said yes. I love how three times Peter denied Jesus yet three times proclaimed his love for Jesus. It's almost as if every yes canceled out every no. Jesus knew Peter's heart; Jesus knew Peter better than Peter knew Peter.

Jesus even gave Peter insight into what the future would hold. Peter would one day end up dying and becoming a martyr for his faith in Jesus. Peter would be crucified when he was in Rome under the Emperor Nero Augustus Caesar. Peter requested to be crucified upside down because he saw himself unworthy of being crucified in the same way as Jesus. When he died, he knew that he couldn't deny Jesus ever again, even if that meant he would be put to death. Peter got to the end of himself. Wow, what a humbling place to be!

THE END OF YOURSELF

Have you ever gotten to the end of yourself? I mean, have you ever gotten to that place in your life where you realize that your own strength isn't enough? I know personally there have been so many times I have allowed my fears, my choices, my sins, and my shortcomings to paralyze me from the blessings God had for me. I think the fear of stepping out in faith and not having much to show for it and the fear of other people's opinions—sometimes even my own—held me back from walking in obedience.

Matthew 5:1–12 is the story of Jesus preaching the Sermon on the Mount. He spoke about when we are blessed: "You're blessed when you're at the end of your rope. With less of you there is more of God and his rule" (Matthew 5:3, MSG). With less of me, there's more of God. That's what each of us ultimately wants, isn't it? We are here today and gone tomorrow, but God is everlasting. I think Peter was at this point when it was his time to go be with the Lord. He knew that he got it wrong the first time when asked if he was with Jesus. Peter couldn't deny Him again. He was willing to die because of what he saw and knew in his heart. Peter finally reached the end of Peter. In Romans 5:1-5 (NIV), it says,

> Therefore, since we have been justified through faith, we have peace with God through our Lord Jesus Christ, through whom we have gained access by faith into this grace in which we now stand. And we boast in the hope of the glory of God. Not only so, but we also glory in our sufferings, because we know that suffering produces perseverance; perseverance, character; and character, hope. And hope does not put us to shame, because God's love has been poured out into our hearts through the Holy Spirit, who has been given to us.

That's what Peter finally understood when he reached the end of himself.

We only get to the end of ourselves when we realize that we can't do it all by ourselves, that we do indeed need a Savior. We need grace, forgiveness, love, joy, peace, patience, kindness, goodness, faithfulness, gentleness, and self-control in our lives. When we accept the truth and see the need of a Savior, we see breakthrough and an overflow of blessings come into our lives. We see positive change, regardless of the chaos going on around us.

FAITH WALKIN'

I've been in ministry now for over twelve years. During this amazing journey in ministry, God has asked me to do some unbelievably crazy faith walks. When thinking and praying about what I should share in this chapter, God brought to my memory the time that I quit my job as the associate children's pastor to take an unpaid, volunteer position.

At that time, the children's pastor and youth pastor wanted to start a preteen ministry at our church. They wanted a way to detach the fifth graders from children's ministry and attach them to the sixth graders in youth ministry. They wanted to build confidence within these two grades to really prepare them for youth ministry. When hearing about the opportunity, I immediately got excited because I absolutely love the preteen stage! I call it the "ugly duckling" stage because those ages are so confusing: your body is changing, and you're making choices about the people you are going to hang out with and the direction you really want to go in life.

After hearing about this opportunity, I went home to my husband and talked it over with him. We both were scared because this position would mean that I would be giving up my paid, comfortable job and working for FREE! I asked my parents for their thoughts, and they weren't too keen on the idea of me losing a paid position to take a volunteer position. I fought God on it a few days. I even asked Him to give me signs if I was really supposed to do this.

Now, even though I was on staff as the associate children's pastor, I didn't know what the sermons were going to be about on Sundays in the adult part of service. Can you guess what the sermon was about the Sunday before I needed to put my name in the hat for the volunteer position for preteen pastor? It was about faith and stepping out of the boat like Peter to go where God calls you to go! When I saw the title of the sermon, I laughed out loud.

I went home after church, and I told my husband, "I really think I'm supposed to do this! I know it's scary, but I can't shake the feeling that God will take care of us and this volunteer position will become a paid position." After much prayer and confirmation from my husband, I went to work the next day and told the pastors that if they felt that I was the right fit for the job, even though it was volunteer, I would love the opportunity and would give up my paid position as associate children's pastor. So, they gave me the go-ahead.

And you know what? Because of God's goodness and faithfulness, we didn't financially struggle while I worked for free and waited for a paycheck that might never come. Within the first two weeks of the job, God told different people to write me a check, and they filled in the financial gap. God didn't let us struggle because we were obedient. He provided for us!

I'll never forget the first Wednesday night that we had for the fifth-and sixth-grade ministry. We had sixty-five students come, and they were so excited to have a program that kept the fifth graders from being bored in children's ministry and the sixth graders from feeling the pressure of being around older kids. They had a program at church that was custom-made for their age group. When the pastors saw the success of the ministry, which was 100% God's hand, they came to tell me that they wanted to go ahead and pay me. It took less than a month for this volunteer position to become a paid position. It was one of those times when I love to use that expression: BUT GOD! God always makes a way where there seems to be no way. God can do the impossible any time and any way He wants, and He invites us to reap the blessing! All we have to do is say yes and believe. God does the rest!

NO FEAR

It is truly amazing how much clarity you have when you get to the end of you. Peter got to the end of himself. He saw the need for Christ in his life. He knew that even in his weakness and fears, God's strength would help him overcome and live out his purpose of preaching the good news of Jesus. He didn't allow any label define him. He knew that God was the One who defined him.

God wants you to know that truth in your life. He wants you to be freed from the label, whatever it may be. Maybe you have labeled yourself by speaking fear over your life. But I can tell you that God's grace is sufficient in every way. He wants you to know that the only label you need to accept is "God's Child." You are His. He loves you. He wants you. He calls you by name, and He had your face on His mind when He hung on the cross. He died for you. Don't walk in fear anymore, walk in faith.

FOCUS VERSES

Look to the Lord and his strength; seek his face always. 1 Chronicles 16:11, NIV

It is God who arms me with strength and keeps my way secure. Psalm 18:32, NIV

God is our refuge and strength, an ever-present help in trouble. Psalm 46:1, NIV

When I am afraid, I put my trust in you. Psalm 56:3, NIV

For the Spirit God gave us does not make us timid but gives us power, love and self-discipline. 2 Timothy 1:7, NIV

QUESTIONS FOR REFLECTION

1. In what ways do I relate to Peter?

_____

_____

_____

2. What fears do I have that keep me from following God?

_____

_____

_____

3. In what areas of my life do I need to get to the end of myself?

_____

_____

_____

4. How can God use me and the struggles I have overcome to help others with similar struggles?

_____

_____

_____

PRAYER

After you ask yourself these questions, pray and ask God to deliver you from your fears:

"Dear God, thank you for forgiving me. Thank you for not giving up on me. Help me not to be overwhelmed by temporary setbacks and situations in my life. Help me walk in faith not fear. Help me be bold and courageous in all areas of my life. I know that you are on my side, Lord, and I don't have to be afraid. Amen."

CHAPTER 8

God Uses the Worrier: Martha

Luke 10:38–42 and John 11:1–44

Martha. Martha. Martha. I wanted to write this chapter about Martha because I can relate to her, as I'm sure many of you probably can, too. Like Martha, I am a worrywart. I want to be transparent with you about this struggle of worry in my life. It has been one of my biggest battles. My sweet husband has been patient on so many occasions when I've repeated myself a million different ways, a million different times, in an attempt to settle my anxious and worrying heart. I have wasted so much time in my life thinking over the "what-if's." And about 90% of the "what-if's" I worry about don't even happen! I even worry about worrying! I'm not joking, either. Many people have this same struggle. But God can use us, even in our frailties and shortcomings, and help us to overcome.

THE HOSTEST WITH THE MOSTEST

Martha was one of those people who probably opened her home to people constantly, and she wanted to be the hostess with the mostest. When Jesus came to her house, she was so busy trying to serve her guests and make them comfortable that she became worried and frustrated with her sister, Mary, because Mary wasn't helping her at all.

We all know one of those people like Mary, right? They come and just chill. They reap the blessing of your labor. That's all they want to do. However, Mary wasn't trying to just come and chill; she wanted to hear and hold onto every word Jesus spoke.

Until Jesus got her attention, Martha didn't realize that she was concerned with things that don't really matter or last in the end: "'Martha, Martha,' the Lord answered, 'you are worried and upset about many things, but few things are needed—or indeed only one. Mary has chosen what is better, and it will not be taken away from her'" (Luke 10:41–42, NIV).

I can totally understand how Martha wanted everything to be just right for guests who came into her house. Yes, it's true, I can be a little bit of a clean freak and germaphobe myself. Since day one, my husband and I have always used our home as a place of ministry. We have hosted everything from small groups to bible studies to prayer groups. I always go into hyper-mode when people are coming over. It never fails—I always do it! I have to make sure that the house smells good, there's not a speck of dust, everything is wiped clean, toilets are cleaned, floors are swept and mopped, and the trash is taken out.

As I have gotten older, I have come to realize that those details aren't really that important. I mean, don't get me wrong, I absolutely want a clean house because it makes me feel calmer when things are cleaned up. And we've all heard the expression "cleanliness is next to godliness." But people aren't really as concerned with how tidy your house: they want to know that you care about them. They want to know that the time they spend with you is valued, not routine or for a show. People crave realness in relationships.

What Jesus was telling Martha was that Mary wasn't trying to be lazy or rude by not helping her. She was wanting a personal relationship with Jesus. That personal relationship outshines any clean house or anything in this world!

CONTROL FREAK

As it is with most worriers, Martha was also a control freak. Instead of fully trusting God, she let her worries overcome her to the point that she wanted to take control of the situation.

Martha and Mary had a brother named Lazarus. Jesus loved the three of them very much. Lazarus became ill and died. When they learned that Jesus was coming to see them after the loss of their brother, Mary chose to stay home, but Martha, with her control-freak self, had to rush out and meet Jesus as He was coming along.

"'Lord,' Martha said to Jesus, 'if you had been here, my brother would not have died. But I know that even now God will give you whatever you ask'" (John 11:21, NIV).

Martha straight up called Jesus out in front of everyone. Not only did she call Him out, but she also told Him that He could ask God to bring her brother back to life. She was frustrated and basically questioned His delay but also recognized Jesus' power. She was having a battle between her flesh and her spirit.

Sound familiar? I know I have had the same battle. Out of my mouth come praises and truth, and out of the same mouth I speak fear and doubt. I have even questioned God multiple times, multiple times a day!

I love the scriptures that follow Martha questioning God in John 11:24–27: "Jesus said to her, 'I am the resurrection and the life. The one who believes in me will live, even though they die; and whoever lives by believing in me will never die. Do you believe this?' 'Yes, Lord,' she replied, 'I believe that you are the Messiah, the Son of God, who is to come into the world.'"

These scriptures show me that Jesus says whoever believes in Him doesn't have to wait for the resurrection because Jesus is the resurrection and the life. Despite our continuous double-mind of trust and worry, He is our constant rock and salvation. He is ALL we need.

HIS WAYS ARE HIGHER

My husband and I are completely opposite in so many ways. We both took a personality test, and it showed that I'm 92% feelings and my husband is 95% logic. I understand completely now why God put my husband and me together. We help each other with our weaknesses, and we even each other out.

If God told me to jump out of a boat, I would say: "Sure!" I would ask twenty-million questions on the way down, but I would still jump! My husband is the one who would try to figure out every detail and connect all the dots before jumping off the boat. It has to make sense to him.

For many of us, it's not logical to trust. However, God doesn't think the way we do, and He definitely doesn't do what we would do: "As the heavens are higher than the earth, so are my ways higher than your ways and my thoughts than your thoughts" (Isaiah 55:9, NIV). We are limited, and as a result, our vision is often blurred or blinded. We can't always trust our own logic, but we can trust the God who sees it all.

As far as my calling goes, I can honestly tell you that it is an exhausting battle when I try to make sense of everything. It makes the journey even harder when I overthink and worry. But when I step out in bold faith and cling to God's word as my guide, everything falls together in a way that I couldn't even have planned.

DON'T WORRY, BE HAPPY

My momma, bless her heart, is a worrier, too. She understands my struggle. When I was growing up, my mom would remind me every day before I left for school: "Put a smile on your face, put God in your heart, and have a happy day today!" She even bought one of those fish that hangs on the wall and sings the "Don't Worry, Be Happy" song. My mom helped me realize that every day I can smile because God is for me. Regardless of the craziness this world brings, God is always with me. He's always with you, too. As Christians, we know that God is with us, but I think sometimes we don't fully believe it.

Having a friendship with my mom as an adult has been one of the biggest joys in my life. What I love about our relationship is the transparency and realness between us. My mom meets me where I am and is always transparent with where she is. We have shared so many laughs, stories, and struggles. We pray for each other and speak truth to help each other when we are too focused on our worries and doubts. We remind each other that nothing in this world is too big for God to handle. I always have and always will look up to my mom.

Knowing that a woman of God like my mom still has similar struggles, I realize that I'm not weird or stupid for feeling the way I do at times. I'm human. Just like my mom and every single person, I need a Savior in my life to save me from myself and the confusion and brokenness of this world.

MY GRANDPA, MY HERO

My grandpa will always be one of my heroes. He was one of those people everyone wanted to be around. He was extremely funny and loving. He was brilliant and business savvy. He didn't compromise his thoughts. We all had a deep respect for him because of his strength, realness, and authenticity.

When I was a junior in high school, my grandpa was hospitalized for congestive heart failure. I was at work, and I remember my boss letting me off early because I was worrying so much about my grandpa that I wasn't productive at all. I was probably more of a distraction.

The next day I went to work again, still worrying of course, and my grandpa had my mom call me at my job so he could talk to me. I answered the phone and heard his sweet, calm voice say to me, "Carri, I'll be okay. You stop being such a worrywart. I love you, bay-beh." My grandpa gave all his kids and grandkids nicknames. I was the youngest grandchild, so I got the name "baby," only he insisted on saying it "bay-beh." See, my sweet grandpa didn't want me to worry—he didn't want anyone to worry. I remember having tears go down my cheeks and telling him that I loved him, too. Even on his deathbed, he wasn't thinking about himself. He was thinking about others.

My grandpa died a couple of days later.

On the night of his passing, my grandpa was talking to my grandma in the hospital room. As he was laying there, he told her that he loved her and thanked her for not only loving him but for being his very best friend for sixty-three years. She told him that she loved him and thanked him for being her very best friend. They both went to sleep peacefully. Grandpa wasn't worried because he knew Jesus. And while he was sleeping, he ran into the arms of his Savior.

I SURRENDER

I don't know if you have ever experienced a panic attack, but it is literally one of the worst experiences I've ever had. You feel as though you can't breathe, and everything is crumbling around you. You feel like nobody and nothing can help you in that moment. Sometimes it hits you out of nowhere. But I've come to understand that for me, it doesn't come out of nowhere: worry, anxiety, and panic build up over time when I don't surrender these feelings to God.

In Matthew 6:34 (NIV), Jesus says: "Therefore do not worry about tomorrow, for tomorrow will worry about itself. Each day has enough trouble of its own." Sometimes it's easier said than done. Worrying comes naturally to my flesh. But what is better for my flesh and my spirit is the complete opposite. I need to trust God. I need to surrender to Him. I need to praise Him. I have to remind myself of these truths daily.

When worry tries to sneak back in, I have to ask God to transform my thoughts: "Do not conform to the pattern of this world, but be transformed by the renewing of your mind. Then you will be able to test and approve what God's will is—his good, pleasing and perfect will" (Romans 12:2, NIV). All worry does is rob me of peace. But if I lay my worries at Christ's feet, then peace overflows in my life. Worry has no room to stay if I don't allow it.

Jesus says we can overcome: "I have told you these things, so that in me you may have peace. In this world you will have trouble. But take heart! I have overcome the world!" (John 16:33, NIV).

We can overcome worry.

We can overcome our need to control.

We can overcome fears.

We can overcome doubts.

Jesus is our strength to overcome!

As I've done a lot of healing in my life, the panic attacks have died down. I have been trying to be intentional about dealing with the things that cause me to be anxious. I'm still definitely a work in progress.

FOCUSING ON YOUR "WHY"

I truly think God gives us the story of Martha to help us understand that in this world there will be things that try to distract us from our focus, which, in turn, cause us to start worrying about things that don't really matter in the end. God wants us to be more of a Mary than a Martha because He wants us to understand that it's more important to give God our focus than things that don't last. God wants us to trust and seek Him always.

More than anything else, knowing what my "why" is has helped me overcome my worries. By my "why," I mean, "Why do I do the things that I do? What is my purpose?" If it's only for my benefit, then surely it will not last, but if it's for God, then it not only will last, but no one will be able to take it away. My "why" is to be a loving, encouraging, motivating, loud, and bold voice for God everywhere I go. It's to make others smile and laugh. It took me some time to have clarity on my "why" because I kept trying to take the steering wheel. Again, I'm a control freak in my own way. But because God is a patient God, He has given me clarity.

Now that I have understood my "why," I also have a clearer understanding of what God wants me to do as well as the gifts and talents that God has given to equip me. I am passionate about speaking, acting, and writing—those things are my "what." My "what" includes all the ways in which I will accomplish my "why."

When my focus gets off of my own goals or desires, I tend to worry less, even to the point where I'm not worrying at all. I'm able to breathe easier. When my gaze is truly on Jesus, I'm able to do the impossible, not because of my strength, but because of God's. The bottom line is this: Stop being a worrywart! Trust God, and press into Him and His word for clarity!

FOCUS VERSES

"You will seek me and find me when you seek me with all your heart." Jeremiah 29:13, NIV

"Therefore do not worry about tomorrow, for tomorrow will worry about itself. Each day has enough trouble of its own." Matthew 6:34, NIV

Do not be anxious about anything, but in every situation, by prayer and petition, with thanksgiving, present your requests to God. Philippians 4:6, NIV

Cast all your anxiety on him because he cares for you. 1 Peter 5:7, NIV

QUESTIONS FOR REFLECTION

1. In what areas of my life do I need to stop worrying?

_____

_____

_____

2. What things have I tried to control that I need to lay at God's feet?

_____

3. What is my "why," (my purpose)?

_____

_____

_____

4. What is my "what," (the ways in which I will accomplish my "why")?

_____

_____

_____

PRAYER

After you ask yourself these questions, pray and ask God to deliver you from your worries:

"Dear God, help me understand my "why" so that I can fully understand my "what" and go toward the things that you want me to do. Help me stop worrying and start submitting to your will, Lord. Give me wisdom to understand how to lay it all down at your feet. Give me peace in the areas that I have no peace. Thank you for being patient with me, Lord. Amen."

CHAPTER 9

God Uses the Hypocrite: Paul

Acts 7–9

Paul wrote a majority of the New Testament and was a full-blown missionary, but he was thought of as a hypocrite early on in his ministry and also admitted to being a hypocrite. What is a hypocrite? By definition, it is a person whose actions don't match his or her spoken beliefs. And guess what?

The person who is writing this book is a hypocrite.

And the person reading this book is a hypocrite, too.

Some of you might be doing a double-take because of what I just said. You're probably thinking, "Wait, did she really just say that?" The answer is yes! I totally did! I'm simply speaking the truth, and sometimes the truth hurts. God still wants to use you, He wants to use me, and He used Paul to do amazing things for Him and His glory.

CHRISTIAN KILLER TURNED CHRISTIAN

Paul, known at this time by the name Saul, was very educated and religiously trained. He devoutly followed Jewish law. He was a know-it-all and a bit of a hot-head. You know the expression "my way or the highway"—yeah, that was Saul.

Saul was the ringleader of a group of Jews who were persecuting Christians. He thirsted for the blood of anyone who proclaimed Jesus to be Lord and Savior. His reputation was, indeed, "The Christian Killer." In fact, he once held people's coats while they stoned and killed a man named Stephen for believing in Jesus Christ and professing Him to be the Lord of Lords. Before Jesus got a hold of Saul, he was convinced that the way he was living was 100% correct.

Let me tell you about the beginning of Saul's transformation. Saul had just received arrest warrants from the chief priest to go and arrest Christ-followers. As he was on his journey to Damascus along with some of his Christ-follower-hating buddies, they heard a voice and Saul was blinded by a bright light. It was the Lord, and He said, "Saul, Saul, why do you persecute me?"

Saul and his buddies were probably thinking, "What to the what?" It's like one of those moments during a television show or a movie when something completely unexpected and powerful happens, and you are asking yourself, "What in the world would I do in this moment? Freeze Up? Pee my pants?" And then it goes to commercial, and you're like, NO!!!!!!

Jesus said to Saul in Acts 9:5 (NIV), "I am Jesus, whom you are persecuting . . . Now get up and go into the city, and you will be told what you must do." Now, if I were Saul in that particular moment, I would be thinking to myself, "Seriously? I played a role in killing followers of Christ because I was believing and teaching a false truth. I was in the wrong. I have put people in jail for worshiping the One who just caused me to go blind. What have I done?" All hope would seem to be lost. Man, what a moment that must have been for Saul, to be blind but to finally see.

Have you ever faced a moment like that, where you felt like the blindfold that you wore confidently for so long came off? Your eyes were opened in a new way that you never thought possible, that you never knew was true.

The Lord then went to Ananias and told him that he must go and baptize Saul and tell him that God was going to use him to do big things for Jesus' name. Now, if I were Ananias I would probably be thinking, "REALLY? ARE YOU KIDDING ME, GOD?" That's basically what Ananias did. He started listing the many reasons why Saul must be the wrong one. Surely God was confused. (Sidenote: God is never confused. Like ever. Like never. He's always right. Period.)

When Ananias stopped arguing with God and went on his way to see Saul, Saul was in Damascus waiting at a house, completely blind. Ananias put his hands on Saul and told Saul that he was sent by Jesus, that he was there to help Saul see again, and that Saul would be filled with the Holy Spirit.

As Ananias was saying these words, scales fell from Saul's eyes. Can you imagine having something similar to fish scales fall out of your eyes? Two words: that's nasty. But hey, it happened. After the scales fell off, Saul stood up and was baptized. It was such an eye-opening moment for Saul, no pun intended—okay, maybe a little.

After Saul accepted Jesus as his Lord and Savior, Saul's life became dramatically different. He began boldly and courageously preaching in Jesus' name. He even switched his name to Paul. His complete turn-around is one of the things I most love and admire about him. He didn't quit. He wasn't perfect, but he was willing. He knew that the God who caused him to go blind and made him see would also be the God who would go before him, to elevate his voice so that the truth would spread like wildfire.

As you can imagine, this change was hard for people to accept at first. Many Christians thought he was trying to trap them. He was going against all the beliefs he was known for, and everyone must have thought he was the ultimate hypocrite.

NO LOOKING BACK

When I was in high school, I went through a stage of rebellion. I was rebelling against God, against my parents, and against the rules. I wanted a taste of what the world had to offer. I gained a little bit of a reputation among my peers because of certain choices I was making. Because of the choices I had made with a boyfriend, rumors were spread about me. When I finally realized that the world's way only left me heartbroken and empty, I chose to change my life and live for God instead of living for myself.

I remember one day in particular. I had brought my Bible with me to school, and I was sitting in one of my classes reading it. Two boys in my class were looking at me, pointing and laughing. One of them said to me, "Yeah, you're sitting there reading your Bible, but we know who you really are."

My heart completely broke, and I was devastated. I even had brief thoughts of suicide again. I could feel the depression try to rise up in my spirit. All I wanted to do in that moment was go home and scream and cry into my pillow out of shame and anger. I thought to myself, "Can I really change my life? Can I make a difference because of the person I used to be? What if everyone looks at me like I'm a hypocrite?" For a brief moment, Satan whispered lies into my heart: "You can't change. You can't be used because you messed up so badly. You'll always be known for what you've done." But I tell you, THE DEVIL IS A LIAR!

After class was over, I pulled those boys into the hallway, and as people were passing by, I spread my arms out wide and yelled as loudly as I could with tears in my eyes, "When Jesus Christ spread His arms out wide, He forgave every single sin! Every sin! He's already forgiven me and my sins." Later one of those boys came back and apologized, but the other didn't.

I admire how Paul ran toward Christ and never looked back after he had his encounter with Jesus. It was not only a huge leap of faith but also a really, really bold move on his part. Paul's reputation was completely against this new way of life. My own reputation was hurt temporarily because of my bad choices. But when I started going toward Christ, I ran toward Him and didn't look back. That doesn't mean I didn't mess up along the way. I totally did. Multiple times. I still do. But I'll tell you, when you have honestly and truly given your heart to Jesus, the Holy Spirit's small still voice is clearer and much harder to ignore.

A LITERAL TUG OF WAR

Even after Paul came to know Jesus, he still struggled, just like we all do. He had a bold personality that sometimes caused problems. In Acts 15:30–41, we see how he got into disagreement with the disciple Barnabas, and they parted ways. Have you ever been in a disagreement with a fellow believer? It's hard, isn't it? You almost want to pray and ask God to take your side, but from God's perspective you're both His kids and He doesn't have favorites or picks sides. He is a fair judge. He is a good Father who disciplines His children by correcting them and redirecting them.

Paul writes about his struggle with sin in Romans 7:14–25 (NIV):

> We know that the law is spiritual; but I am unspiritual, sold as a slave to sin. I do not understand what I do. For what I want to do I do not do, but what I hate I do. And if I do what I do not want to do, I agree that the law is good. As it

is, it is no longer I myself who do it, but it is sin living in me. For I know that good itself does not dwell in me, that is in my sinful nature. For I have the desire to do what is good, but I cannot carry it out. For I do not do the good I want to do, but the evil I do not want to do this I keep on doing. Now if I do what I do not want to do, it is no longer I who do it, but it is sin living in me that does it. So I find this law at work: Although I want to do good, evil is right there with me. For in my inner being I delight in God's law; but I see another law at work in me, waging war against the law of my mind and making me a prisoner of the law of sin at work within me. What a wretched man I am! Who will rescue me from this body that is subject to death? Thanks be to God, who delivers me through Jesus Christ our Lord! So then, I myself in my mind am a slave to God's law, but in my sinful nature a slave to the law of sin.

Paul was saying that even when he wants to do good, his flesh and sin get the best of him. There's a literal tug of war between good and evil in each of us: it's our spirit versus our flesh. Every single person has this same struggle. We know what we ought to do but choose to do things our way and in our timing because we think we are higher up in the wisdom department than God. Feeling convicted? I know that I am!

I could seriously highlight every single word in the book of Romans. Romans is one of my most favorite books in the Bible. You can see the passion that Paul is expressing to the people in

Rome. He wanted them to fully understand God's grace. He wanted them to understand that even when they fall short, God's grace covers a multitude of sins.

MY OWN TUG OF WAR

I think each of us can relate to Paul on so many levels. When you have really submitted to God and your heart wants to follow Christ, your life should look dramatically different. No, I didn't say perfect. We aren't Jesus. I said different.

For me, my life without Jesus as my main focus looks totally different than my life with Jesus as my main focus and purpose. Without Jesus it was all about me.

Me.

Me.

Me.

I was selfish. I didn't grasp what it meant to serve. I didn't have the fruits of the Spirit: love, joy, peace, patience, kindness, goodness, faithfulness, gentleness, and self-control. I put up idols that eventually failed me. I put boyfriends before God. I put my friends before God. I had myself on my mind all the time.

With Jesus, it's all about Him.

Jesus.

Jesus.

Jesus.

Now I have God on my mind all the time. I know that I can't do anything without Him. Because of Jesus, my marriage and parenting is Christ-centered. I hang out with a different crowd. I make sure that I surround myself with women who challenge me in my walk to develop a closer relationship with God. My encounters with other people have changed because now I want others to know the truth and hope that I cling to daily.

I still fall short. Each of us will. I am the biggest hypocrite when it comes to diet. I know without a doubt what I should do to get healthy. I have even preached to women's groups about eating healthy and exercising. I am constantly doing a yo-yo act with my weight because it has been one of my biggest struggles. I've always told myself, "I guess I don't have the self-discipline to overcome this obstacle of weight and diet in my life," knowing good and well that's a lie because it took a lot of discipline for me to sit down and write this book. Self-control is a fruit of the Spirit. Because of Jesus in me, I'm capable of self-control. I know that with God I will overcome! God has the last word.

THE HARD TRUTH ABOUT MANY CHRISTIANS

It saddens me to watch a television show or a movie with a Christian character who is so far from what a Christ-follower should look like. You know what I'm talking about: those goody-goody, gossipy, cliquey, judgy, arrogant "Christians" who think that the world revolves around them and that they are better than everyone else, especially anyone who sins differently than they do. Oh wait, the hard truth is THAT'S WHAT MANY CHRISTIANS LOOK LIKE!

When we give into our flesh, that's what we look like—harsh, but unfortunately, true. We brag about ourselves instead of the One who deserves all glory, honor, and praise. We are prideful about our gifts and talents, and we forget to thank the One who gave them to us in the first place. We use them to get a following on social media for ourselves instead of a following for Jesus. We go to our friends and tell them gossip, but we translate it into a prayer request, so it doesn't look like gossip. We act like it's our job to be the judge, jury, and executioner when we should be guiding our fellow Christian brothers and sisters back on the right path with the love that Christ has called us to show. We sit with our friends at church, and we choose to worship in comfort instead of reaching out to someone we don't know, someone who might be different than we are. We care about what songs the band plays during worship, and if they don't sing our favorite songs, we get upset. After all, worship is all about us, right? WRONG! We want to sit in the air conditioning, and we want church to be about our wants and needs. WHO ARE WE? We are here today and gone tomorrow. God is and will always be. Unfortunately, we as Christ-followers have shown the world our shortcomings.

We have the power through Christ to change the world's perception of Christians. Let's get to the end of ourselves and allow Christ to shine through our shortcomings. It starts with you; it starts with me. We have the ability to make a change.

HOPE FOR US ALL

If you feel any conviction over what you just read, please know that you aren't alone. I'm the one typing these words, and I feel completely and utterly convicted. But again, I want you to understand that the purpose of this chapter isn't to condemn you or to point fingers at you. It is, however, is to encourage you.

There's hope for us all. God took a headstrong man who was 100% religious-minded instead of being relationship-minded and made him one of the boldest voices for Christ there ever was. If God can transform someone like Paul, surely God can transform us, too. If God can use someone who literally hunted and killed Christ-followers, then God can use a misfit hypocrite like me and like you.

Regardless of your past, regardless of your choices, regardless of your mistakes, God loves you. He wants to use you to do amazing and mighty things for Him. I know, I believe, that if we would set our gaze on Jesus without looking back, our lives would grow to reflect the One whom we love and serve, and the world would see us in a much different light.

FOCUS VERSES

Even youths grow tired and weary, and young men stumble and fall; but those who hope in the Lord will renew their strength. They will soar on wings like eagles; they will run and not grow weary, they will walk and not be faint. Isaiah 40:30-31, NIV

Jesus answered them, "It is not the healthy who need a doctor, but the sick. I have not come to call the righteous but sinners to repentance." Luke 5:31, NIV

When Jesus spoke again to the people, he said, "I am the light of the world. Whoever follows me will never walk in darkness, but will have the light of life." John 8:12, NIV

At this they covered their ears and, yelling at the top of their voices, they all rushed at him, dragged him out of the city and began to stone him. Meanwhile, the witnesses laid their coats at the feet of a young man named Saul. Acts 7:56-57, NIV

But the Lord said to Ananias, "Go! This man is my chosen instrument to proclaim my name to the Gentiles and their kings and to the people of Israel. I will show him how much he must suffer for my name." Acts 9:15-16, NIV

Therefore, if anyone is in Christ, the new creation has come: The old has gone, the new is here! 2 Corinthians 5:17, NIV

QUESTIONS FOR REFLECTION

1. How do I relate to Paul's story?

_____

_____

_____

2. What part of this chapter spoke to me the most, and why?

_____

_____

_____

3. What does Romans 8:6 mean to me?

_____

_____

_____

4. In what areas of my life have I fallen short and need God's help?

_____

_____

_____

PRAYER

After you ask yourself these questions, pray and ask God to deliver you from hypocrisy:

"Dear God, I have fallen short. I have been a hypocrite. Help me be more like you, Lord. Help me show the world how great you are and how you can totally transform and renew someone, even someone like me. Forgive me for judging those you have called me to love. Help me love with your heart and see with your eyes. Amen."

CHAPTER 10
God Can Use You, Too!

You have officially made it to the last chapter! I don't know if the title of this book grabbed your attention, someone recommended it to you, or you just decided to grab this book on impulse. No matter how you came to pick up this book, I can promise you this: God is trying to get your attention.

God has a purpose and a plan for your life. He wants you to know that if He can use these broken, messed up people—which includes me too—and not only use them but do absolutely amazing things through them, He can use you, too. I hope and pray that stories in this book have encouraged you, motivated you, and inspired you like they have me.

GET INSPIRED!

Joseph inspires me to keep going. He encountered so much, yet he
didn't quit. The other day, I saw a cartoon that hit close to home.
In the cartoon, a guy is using a pick-axe to chisel through dirt and
rocks to get to these diamonds. It shows him walking away from
hundreds of diamonds when he has only about five or so more
swings left to get to them. But he quit. He threw in the towel. He
was done. He was so very close to the dream. The pain that we feel
when we fall short or mess up is nothing compared to the pain of
knowing what could have been if we hadn't stopped short. When
God gives you dreams, you can't quit just because things get hard.
You have to keep going in spite of the obstacles you face and press
into God every single step of the way. If only that cartoon man
knew what was on the other side of the dirt and rock, he wouldn't
have given up so easily. If God has put a dream in your heart, go
for it!

Gideon's story inspires me because God called him a mighty
warrior even though he was hiding, making excuses, questioning
God, and testing God every step of the way. God called Gideon
according to how He designed Gideon to be. He proved Himself to
Gideon, time and time again. God made it clear that Gideon had no
reason to doubt His goodness and His power, and neither do we!

I am inspired by Naomi to not let the broken pieces of my life
dictate my day-to-day existence and my future. I can't stay in the
brokenness; I need to allow the Sculptor to make a beautiful

mosaic masterpiece out of my broken pieces. I need to use the messy places in my life as a tool to help people in their mess. If I can prevent people from making the same mistakes that I have made in my life, then I want to help others any way I can. Naomi finally got her eyes off of herself and started helping Ruth. We also need to get eyes off of ourselves and be a blessing to those around us. We need to open our hands, let go of the brokenness, and grab someone to help lift them out of their mess. We need to show others that there is life beyond the mess.

David inspires me to not let my past choices and sins hinder me from God's greatness. Yes, I've messed up. I will continue to mess up every single day of my life because I am human. I need God to help me all day, every day. I need God's grace. I want to have a heart after God. How amazing would it be to have a heart after God!

Jonah's story inspires me because it shows me that even when I've chosen the harder road, God will get me to where He is calling me to be. I don't have to overthink and undertrust. I can completely and utterly trust my Savior and His promises. God never breaks His promises. It also shows me that even when I pout because I didn't get my way or things didn't turn out the way I planned or hoped for, that God is still good and faithful. He will meet me in my bad moods and lovingly guide me back to the right path I need to be on. He's so good and faithful that way, even when we don't deserve it. We have to remember that delayed obedience is still disobedience. God wants His children to have a heart that loves Him and is obedient to the call on their lives. As I am writing this book, I'm thirty-one years old and I finally understand that truth.

Peter inspires me to walk in faith and not in fear and shame. God knows everything there is to know about me. He knows all my fears, and He knows when I act in fear instead of faith. If Peter had allowed a rooster crow to keep him from preaching, it would have been an incredible loss. But Peter grew from that rooster crow. He grew so much strength and endurance that when they put him to death through crucifixion, he humbled himself and said that there wasn't any way he was worthy enough to die the way his sweet Savior did, so they crucified him upside down. His faith became rock solid.

I am inspired by Martha to stop being such a "worrywart," as my grandpa would tell me. Worrying doesn't change anything other than my peace. I want to have complete peace. Many think that complete peace isn't obtainable, but that's a lie. God is the only source of complete peace. Every struggle and every obstacle is nothing compared to how big and faithful God is. If we really believe that God has everything in His hands, then why worry?

Paul's story inspires me because he had to rewrite his reputation by earning people's trust and allowing the Holy Spirit to speak through him. Actually, God rewrote Paul's reputation for him. God wanted to use Saul, so he renamed him Paul. God used Paul to do amazing things and even used him to write the majority of the New Testament. Paul was bold in his faith in Jesus. He was definitely a force to be reckoned with.

HOORAY FOR THE UNDERDOG!

My mom spoke these words of wisdom to me one day: "God is going to use people we would never use. God is going to use people we would never choose." God always picks the underdogs and misfits to accomplish incredible things for His namesake.

Some may wonder why He works this way. I think I know why: He does it to show us all that although we might be the last to be picked, overlooked, or undervalued when it comes to the world's standards—but God. But God. But God. God loves to pick the underdogs and misfits to do extraordinary things and show us that through His strength we are able. I love and admire that about my sweet Lord.

Look at the twelve disciples that Jesus picked to be His helpers and inner circle through the journey of His ministry. They were definitely twelve men whom most of us would overlook. But Jesus didn't overlook them. He called them to follow Him, and they did.

Isn't that what we all crave? Believers and unbelievers alike want the underdog to win. We want the least likely to be the ones picked. I think it's because to some extent each of us feels like we are the underdogs, like we aren't good enough. That's why every single superhero ever created was the underdog turned hero in their story.

Believe me, I know more than most people know about superheroes because of my son, Abram. Every superhero has a story of sadness, loss, and defeat. They all believe that they will never accomplish anything great. Every superhero has thoughts of throwing in the towel because of how hard and big their calling is. But they also have a story of overcoming. They become the ones everyone looks up to and the ones everyone else wishes they could be.

THE TOILET-PAPER EXPERIMENT

Some have asked me why I chose to write about these particular people from the Bible. Well, I guess you could say there are parts in all of their stories and struggles that I can relate to in my own story. I've been told so many times that I'm crazy for pursuing writing, public speaking, and acting and that I'm all over the place because I have so many different projects going on at the same time. But I honestly don't care anymore what people think.

One night I did this social experiment at the mall. I was having a girls' night with my best friends. I got a long piece of toilet paper out of the bathroom and stuck it in the back of my pants. I wanted to see what people would do. Now, reading this you are probably thinking to yourself that I have a few screws loose or I'm off my rocker. I'm not going to deny that. I'm 100% goofy, and I'm a youth pastor, so what do you expect?

I walked around the mall for a couple hours, and only three strangers came up to me to tell me I had toilet paper hanging out. The rest of the people would point and laugh. Sad, isn't it? But guess what? It was one of the most freeing experiments because the joke was really on them. It made them look like ignorant jerks. I could walk boldly with a giant smile on my face because I knew what I was doing. I think it freed me to pursue the calling on my life. Now, I only care what my Heavenly Father thinks. After all, God is the One I'll come face to face with when I die to be judged. I won't be judged by the naysayers or ignorant jerks.

If you're daring, I encourage you to try this social experiment out! It really is funny!

NO LONGER MY LIFE BUT YOURS

When I think about what God is calling me to do, I laugh out loud because it makes no sense at all. Like seriously, not at all. God told me to write a book, which I found super funny because growing up, I was horrible at grammar. I know for a fact I made it through high school because of Cliff's Notes and my friend Rachael. When it comes to song writing, I find it ridiculous because I don't even know how to read music anymore. I used to take piano lessons when I was younger but now I don't have any earthly idea which note is what. When I think about public speaking or acting, it's also humorous because I got a D in drama class. I was too afraid to speak in front of people. I was so afraid of what others would think of me that I would be paralyzed with fear.

Some people, actually many people, would probably say that they had no idea or even believed that I would be doing any of those things. Guess what? By myself, I absolutely wouldn't be able to do any of those things. However, I surrendered to God's will and simply said, "Yes, take me where you want me. It's no longer my life but yours, Jesus." Then God started doing mind-blowing, crazy, amazing things in my life. And He continues to use me in ways I never could have hoped or dreamed. I give Him and Him alone all glory, honor, and praise. I want to be like the servant from the parable in Matthew 25:14–30, the one who used and multiplied the gifts, not the one who buried the one gift and never saw any fruit.

A LEGACY OF FAITH

God wants you to open your heart up to Him and seek Him. Maybe you've been in a dark place for some time. Maybe you've allowed your choices and other's choices to dictate how you live your life. Stop settling for a life of bondage and open your heart to live freely as God intended you to live. God didn't send His One and Only Son Jesus to die on a cross so that you can just settle for less. Stop wasting your life away. He wants you to experience blessings and freedom this side of Heaven. Yes, you'll be able to experience it when you go to Heaven, but you can also experience that amazing freedom now! So, why not?

As I serve in ministry, I cling to this verse from Hebrews 6:10 (NIV): "God is not unjust; he will not forget your work and the love you have shown him as you have helped his people and continue to help them." I want to love and encourage people. I want to honor God with every breath I take. I want to go where God calls me to go, even if it doesn't make sense.

I can promise you this: I am not going to quit. I don't want to be like that cartoon man who gives up before reaching the promise. I will keep at it every day until the Lord calls me home. I want to look my children in the eyes with full confidence and tell them that Mommy trusted God and will continue to do so regardless of the craziness, confusion, and brokenness of this life. I want to lay down a foundation for my family that will inspire them to remain faithful to God and go further than I did long after I'm gone and with my Savior in heaven. That's my heart. That's my focus. That's my vision. That's the legacy I want to leave, and I'm going to leave.

What do you want to do? How do you want to be remembered? What impact do you want to make on those around you? What is your legacy going to be? Remember, God wants to use you! No more excuses! Get ready! Go! Go! Go!

FOCUS VERSES

"I am the true vine, and my Father is the gardener. He cuts off every branch in me that bears no fruit, while every branch that does bear fruit he prunes so that it will be even more fruitful. You are already clean because of the word I have spoken to you. Remain in me, as I also remain in you. No branch can bear fruit by itself; it must remain in the vine. Neither can you bear fruit unless you remain in me." John 15:5-6, NIV

"If you remain in me and my words remain in you, ask whatever you wish, and it will be done for you. This is to my Father's glory, that you bear much fruit, showing yourselves to be my disciples." John 15:7-8, NIV

And we know that in all things God works for the good to those who love him, who have been called according to his purpose. Romans 8:28, NIV

I press on toward the goal to win the prize for which God has called me heavenward in Christ Jesus. Philippians 3:14, NIV

QUESTIONS FOR REFLECTION

1. Which chapter of this book touched my heart the most, and why?

_____

_____

_____

2. What abuses, doubts, brokenness, sins, unwillingness, fears, worry, hypocrisy or other issues do I have that have made me think I can't be used by God? No more excuses! What am I going to lay down at Christ's feet so that I can do what He has called me to do?

_____

_____

_____

3. What has God been wanting me to do?

_____

_____

_____

4. What changes am I going to make today to go where God wants me to go?

_____

_____

_____

PRAYER

After you ask yourself these questions, pray and ask God to use you in whatever way He wills:

"Dear God, thank you for giving me a different perspective. Thank you for being so full of grace that you forgive the unforgivable and love the unlovable. You are truly an amazing God. Help me go where you have called me. Help me be the woman or man you have called me to be. Amen.

87652490R00086

Made in the USA
Columbia, SC
25 January 2018